CONFIDENTIAL.

For the use of Battery Commanders.
Not to be taken into first line trenches.

R.L.

HANDBOOK

OF

AMMUNITION.

This issue is made in substitution of Handbook bearing date January, 1917. All copies of previous issue now in possession should be destroyed.

MAY, 1918.

www.fireteppublishing.com

FireStep Publishing
Gemini House
136-140 Old Shoreham Road
Brighton
BN3 7BD

www.firesteppublishing.com

First published by the General Staff, War Office 1918.
First published in this format by FireStep Editions,
an imprint of FireStep Publishing, in association with
the National Army Museum, 2013.

www.nam.ac.uk

ISBN 978-1-908487-59-9

Cover design FireStep Publishing
Typeset by FireStep Publishing
Printed and bound in Great Britain

Please note: *In producing in facsimile from original historical documents, any imperfections may be reproduced and the quality may be lower than modern typesetting or cartographic standards.*

CONFIDENTIAL.

For the use of Battery Commanders.
Not to be taken into first line trenches.

R.L.

HANDBOOK

OF

AMMUNITION.

This issue is made in substitution of Handbook bearing date January, 1917. All copies of previous issue now in possession should be destroyed.

MAY, 1918.

NOTES ON FUZES.

FUZES.

Fuzes may be divided into two classes :—

(1). Percussion, designed to act on impact.

(2). Time and Percussion, designed to act in the air after a certain time, or on impact. The percussion mechanism may be omitted when the fuze is required to act as time only.

The former are used generally with H.E. Shell when the object to be attained is the attack of material, such as ships, buildings, or trenches ; while the latter are chiefly used with Shrapnel Shell for the attack of personnel. Shrapnel Shell with time fuze has been found very efficacious for destroying wire entanglements, and under certain conditions H.E. Shell can be employed with effect against personnel.

Some percussion fuzes are designed so that their action is delayed, thus allowing the shell to penetrate for a certain distance into the object which it is desired to destroy, before the shell explodes.

TIME FUZES.

One of the simplest types of time fuze is that originally used with the Stokes' Trench Howitzers, which consists of a length of ordinary "trade" safety fuze, one end of which is attached to an igniting cap.

This fuze is cut to the length required, before assembly in the bomb. The cap is fired by a cocked striker released on shock of discharge.

Time fuzes are generally ignited by the shock of discharge which causes a needle to pierce and fire a fuze detonator or cap. The needle (or detonator) is fitted in a pellet which is held off a detonator (or needle) in the body of the fuze by a spring or stirrup. When the inertia of the shell is overcome on discharge, the pellet tends to remain behind or set back, thus bringing the needle and detonator into contact.

In the French time fuzes, the slow burning composition is contained in a lead tube. The No. 28 time fuze is of this type, in which the fuze is set for the desired time of burning by piercing the lead tube so that it is ignited at a determined point, thus leaving a greater or less length of tube to burn before flashing into the powder filled magazine of the fuze, which in its turn explodes the shell.

The British Service time fuze is of the ring type. The slow burning composition consisting of gunpowder is pressed into a channel milled nearly completely round the under surface of a flat ring. This composition is ignited at a fixed point and burns over the platform of the body, which has at one point a flash hole leading to the magazine. The ring can be rotated so as to cause a greater or smaller length of the composition to burn before the communicating hole into the magazine is reached, enabling the fuze to be set for the time of burning required by means of an index and graduations on the exterior of the movable ring and body.

Most fuzes have two such rings, the upper fixed and the lower movable. The principle is, however, the same, the direction of burning being in opposition.

The percussion portion of time and percussion fuzes is of the graze type. (See below).

As time fuzes are ignited on the shock of discharge, the only safety that need be considered is that required in transit, and for this, either the stirrup or spring supporting the detonator and the needle must be made sufficiently strong to withstand ordinary rough usage, or else a safety pin, removable before loading, must pass between them. The latter is necessary in Howitzers and large guns with which the set back would not be enough to overcome a stirrup or spring of the required strength.

PERCUSSION FUZES.

Percussion fuzes have not only to be safe in transit but also on shock of discharge and during the flight of the projectile. There are three forces which have to be taken into account :—

(1). Set-back.
(2). Centrifugal force.
(3). Creep.

Of these, set-back has been described under time fuzes; centrifugal force is due to the rotation of the projectile and acts radially outwards. It is made use of for purposes of safety, as will be described later ; while creep is the tendency of a pellet in a graze fuze to move forward owing to the retardation of the shell, due to the resistance of the air.

Percussion fuzes may act in either of two ways :—

(1). By Direct Action. In this case the fuze is placed in the nose of the shell and it has either a weak needle disc or a needle pellet which is crushed in, on impact on the target.

With these fuzes the needle disc or pellet is generally sufficiently strongly held (until the tremendous blow on impact) as to render unnecessary any safety device to enable it to withstand shock of discharge. For safety in transit a cap is provided which is removed before loading the shell into the gun.

(2). By Graze Action. In this case the fuze may be either in the nose or base of the shell, and conversely to direct action fuzes, which function by distortion of the fuze, the better protected it is the less likely it is to be adversely affected by distortion on impact. The graze fuze acts by the meeting of a needle and a fuze detonator, one of these elements being placed in a loose pellet which moves forward, when the shell is checked, on to the other element, which is placed in the body of the fuze. Such a graze pellet is often retained in its position, for purposes of safety in transit and loading, by a bolt which is freed from the pellet under the action of centrifugal force. This bolt must generally be retained in position by a further safety device until shock of discharge. This further safety device may either be a detent supported on a strong spring which withdraws on set-back on shock of discharge, as in the No. 100 type of fuze, or also it may be a detent which is pushed inwards by the pressure of the gas of the propellant as in the larger base fuzes.

The action of the forces mentioned are as follows :—

On firing, the shock of discharge or gas pressure releases any detent which may be present, but centrifugal force is, generally speaking, not sufficiently great while the shell is in the bore for a centrifugal mechanism to act against the friction caused by the force of its own set back. The centrifugal mechanism, however, acts almost immediately on the shell leaving the muzzle and after that creep begins to occur. This is generally overcome by interposing a weak spring between the graze pellet and the needle or detonator in the body of the fuze.

It has been found advantageous to add in some cases an extra safety in the shape of a shutter designed to mask the flash from the detonator in case of a premature in the gun. Such a shutter acts by centrifugal force and should, therefore, be operative until the shell has left the bore. The No. 44 D.A. fuze and the shutter in the No. 101E fuze and the new No. 106E fuze are cases in point.

NOTE :—

There is a difference which should be noted between a shell which explodes and one which detonates.

Ordinary gunpowder explodes a shell by the pressure developed by the gas formed as the powder burns, and this is a comparatively slow process, which breaks a shell up into relatively large pieces. Detonation is practically instantaneous conversion of a high explosive into gas, and this breaks the shell up into numerous small fragments with extraordinary rapidity. In order to detonate a high explosive shell it is not sufficient to light it with a flame, as would be sufficient for a powder filled shell, but it is necessary to adopt some special means. These means are either the attachment to an ordinary fuze of a detonating gaine such as the No. 2, which contains a fulminate detonator, or else the assembly of the shell with a true detonating fuze. A detonating fuze differs from an ordinary fuze in that the flame from the detonator of an ordinary fuze may pass down quite a long channel before it ignites the powder magazine or other suitable igniting material, but in the case of a detonating fuze the detonator must itself be of pure fulminate, and there must be a practically continuous channel of a detonating material between the detonator and the detonating composition in the magazine of the fuze. It will thus be seen that a detonating fuze cannot be replaced by an ordinary type of fuze; moreover, a detonating fuze is not a suitable means of firing a powder filled shell, as the detonation of the fuze is apt to break up the shell before the powder has time to burn to a good exploding pressure. This is the reason that the No. 109 fuze, for instance, is used in powder filled shell instead of the No. 101 from which it is converted; the conversion consisting of the substitution of the detonating gaine by a powder relay.

ALLOCATION OF FUZES.

Guns and Howitzers:—

The time and percussion fuzes are used almost entirely in Shrapnel shell, the No. 80, which burns 22 seconds, in the 13 & 18-pr. and A.A. guns, and the Nos. 83 and 87 fuzes, which burn 30 seconds, in larger guns. Shrapnel is rarely used in the 4·5-in. Howitzer for which the No. 82 fuze is approved. The No. 82 fuze may also be used in certain guns to make use of the long range given by its 40 seconds time of burning, in order to attack observation balloons. For this purpose, however, a still longer burning fuze has been introduced.

In the case of anti-aircraft guns, time fuzes are also used in H.E. shell, and have the percussion mechanism removed to prevent the shell bursting on return to the ground if the time arrangement fails to act. These fuzes are distinguished by being known as **"over 44,"** thus the No. 80 T. & P. fuze modified for use in an H.E. shell is known as the 80/44.

Generally speaking, graze fuzes are used with guns and direct action fuzes with Howitzers, except for coast defence purposes, where the guns are provided with direct action fuzes designed to act on thin armour plate.

See pages "Miscellaneous" 11–13 for allocation of fuzes.

Fuze, Time and Percussion, No. 65a.

R.L. Design 20,600.

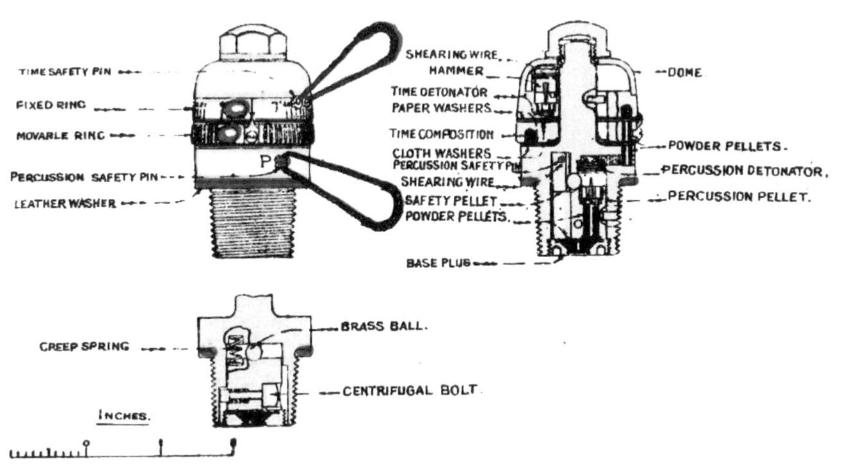

Time of burning, 20 seconds (approx.)

Action of Time Portion.—The fuze is set by unclamping the nut and turning round the lower time ring until the graduation ordered is opposite the pointer on the ring. The nut is then clamped securely. At the moment of loading, the time safety pin is withdrawn and the closing pellet closes up the hole occupied by the pin and so prevents the gas, on discharge, getting into the fuze. On the shock of discharge the hammer in the lighting chamber sets back, shearing its suspending wire, and fires the detonating composition in the bottom of the lighting chamber and ignites the top ring, the brass disc being blown out to allow the gas to escape. The top ring burns round the reverse way to which the shell is rotating until it comes to the powder pellet at the beginning of the lower ring, which is then fired, blowing out the brass disc, and igniting the lower ring. The lower ring burns back the opposite way to the top until it comes to the pellet of powder in the body ; this is fired, and ignites the powder in the horizontal channel, firing the percussion detonator and the bursting charge of the shell.

Action of percussion part.—At the moment of loading the percussion safety pin is withdrawn, the closing pellet closing the hole occupied by the pin. On shock of discharge the safety pellet sets back to the bottom of the slot in the percussion pellet, shearing its suspending wire, the brass ball following it on the first motion of rotation. The spiral spring prevents the percussion pellet rebounding, and the anti-boring pin prevents the pellet from turning.

Owing to the rotation of the shell the heavy end of the centrifugal bolt overpowers the spring and withdraws the smaller end from the recess, so that the percussion pellet is free to move forward, which it does on graze or impact, compressing the spiral spring ; the needle striking the percussion detonator fires the fuze.

Fuze, Time and Percussion, No. 80.

R.L. Design 21,860, etc.

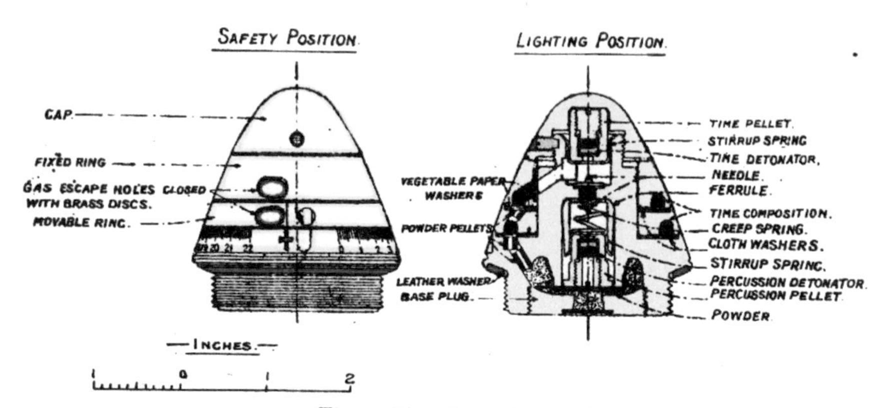

Time of burning, 22 secs. (approx.)

Action of Time portion.—The fuze cover having been removed the fuze is set by turning round the lower time ring by means of the fuze key, or by the setter, until the setting mark on the ring is opposite the graduation ordered. On shock of discharge the time pellet sets back, straightens out the arms of the stirrup spring, and carries its detonator on to the upper point of the needle. The flash from the exploding detonator passes through the hole in the stem communicating with the top ring, and ignites the fuze composition, blowing out the disc covering the gas escape hole. The top ring burns round in the same direction as the spin of the shell until it comes to the exposed powder pellet at the beginning of the lower time ring, which is fired, igniting the lower ring, and blowing out the covering disc for the gas escape hole. The lower ring now burns back the reverse way to the upper ring until it arrives at the powder pellet in the body, which is fired, igniting the powder in the magazine of fuze, and the bursting charge of the shell.

Action of percussion portion.—On shock of discharge the brass ferrule sets back, straightening out the arms of the stirrup spring, and so unmasks the front end of the percussion pellet. The creep spring prevents rebound action on shock of discharge and creeping action during flight. On graze, or impact, the percussion pellet with the ferrule is dashed violently forward, compressing the creep spring, and carries the detonator on to the lower point of the needle. The flash from the exploded detonator passes down through the hole in the screw plug and fires the magazine of the fuze, the flash from which, passing through the hole in the bottom plug, explodes the bursting charge of the shell.

See page 12 for notes *re* other fuzes of No. 80 type.

Fuze, Time and Percussion, No. 82.

R.L. Designs 14,360 S. & 25600.

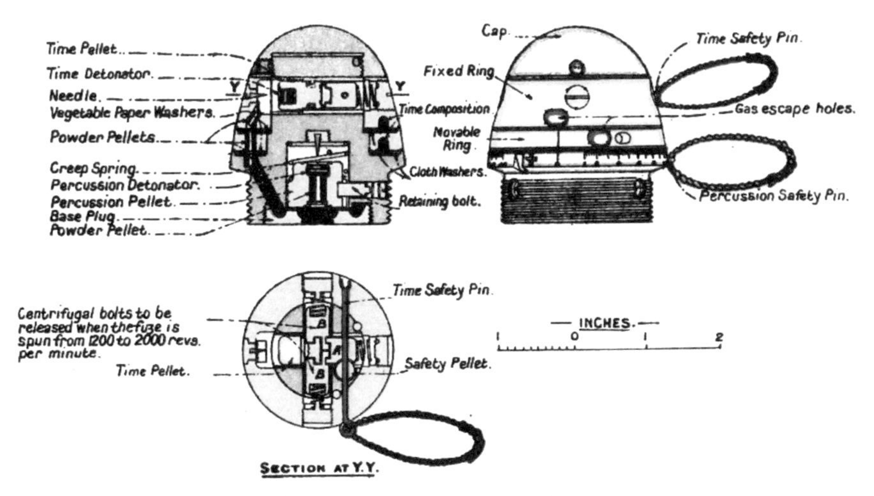

Time of burning 40 secs. (approx.)

Action of time portion.—The fuze having been set to the required graduation, the time safety pin is withdrawn before loading.

On shock of discharge the shearing wire in the safety pellet is broken, and the pellet sets back to the bottom of its recess. In this position the pellet no longer prevents the bolt (A) from moving.

When the shell rotates, the bolt (A) moves outwards and unlocks the other two bolts (BB) ; these now fly outwards and unlock the lighting pellet ; this therefore, flies outwards and carries its detonator on to the needle The flash from the detonator fires the perforated powder pellet below the needle and ignites the upper time ring.

The top ring burns round in the same direction as the spin of rotation until it comes to the exposed powder pellet at the beginning of the lower time ring, which is fired, igniting the lower ring and blowing out the covering disc of the gas escape hole. The lower ring now burns back the reverse way to the upper ring until it arrives at the powder pellet in the body, which is fired, igniting the powder in the magazine and the bursting charge of the shell.

Action of the percussion portion.—At the moment of loading, the percussion safety pin is withdrawn, the closing pellet closing the hole from which the pin has been removed.

On rotation, the retaining bolts of the percussion arrangement are spun out of their recesses in the percussion pellet : the spiral spring prevents any rebound action or tendency for the pellet to creep forward during flight. On graze or impact, the percussion pellet is carried forward, the needle firing the detonator and the perforated powder pellet, the flash from which ignites the magazine of the fuze and the bursting charge of the shell.

Later issues of this fuze are fitted with a screwed in percussion needle.

Fuze, Time and Percussion, No. 83, Mark I.

R.L. Design 17,210 A.

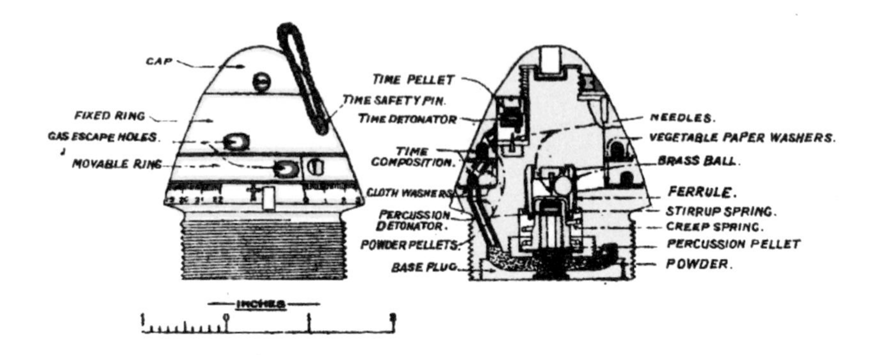

Time of burning, 30 secs. (approx.)

Action of time portion.—The safety pin is removed at the last moment before loading. On the shock of discharge, the time pellet sets back, straightening out the arms of the stirrup spring, and carries the detonator on to the needle. The flash from the exploding detonator ignites the top ring, which burns round the same way as the shell is rotating until it arrives at the perforated powder pellet at the beginning of the lower ring; the lower ring burns back in the opposite direction until it arrives at the perforated powder pellets in the body, which fire the magazine of the fuze and the bursting charge of the shell.

Action of percussion portion.—On shock of discharge, the ferrule sets back, straightening out the arms of its stirrup spring, unmasking the front of the percussion pellet, and releasing the safety ball. The rotary motion of the shell causes the ball to spin out into the recess in the stem, leaving the pellet free to move forward ; the creep spring prevents any rebound action, and also prevents the pellet from creeping forward during flight. On graze or impact, the pellet is carried forward on to the needle, firing the detonator, the magazine of the fuze, and the bursting charge of the shell.

No. 83 Mark II. fuze is similar to above, but has a clamping cap instead of a tensioned cap.

See page No. 9 for latest type of No. 83 fuze, with modified time arrangement, which eliminates the safety pin.

See page 12 for notes *re* other fuzes of No. 83 type.

Fuze, Time and Percussion, No. 83, Mks. III. & IV.

R.L. Designs 23,290 & 26,790.

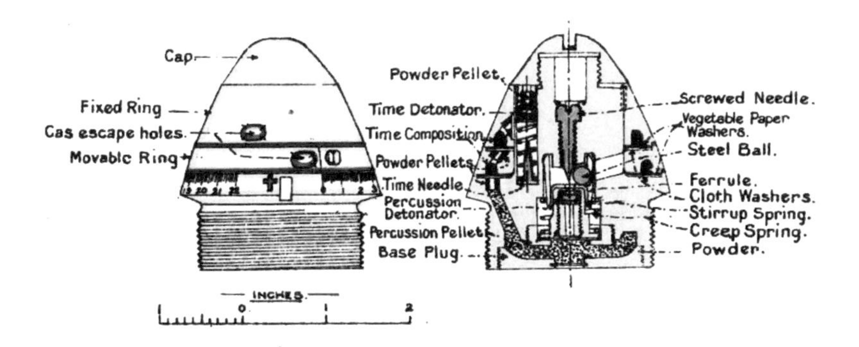

Time of burning, 30 secs. (approx.)

Action of time portion.—On the shock of discharge, the time pellet sets back, overcoming the spiral spring and carrying the detonator on to the needle. The flash from the exploding detonator ignites the top ring, which burns round the same way as the shell is rotating until it arrives at the perforated powder pellet at the beginning of the lower ring; the lower ring burns back in the opposite direction until it arrives at the perforated powder pellets in the body, which fire the magazine of the fuze and the bursting charge of the shell.

Action of percussion portion.—On shock of discharge, the ferrule sets back, straightening out the arms of its stirrup spring, unmasking the front of the percussion pellet, and releasing the safety ball. The rotary motion of the shell causes the ball to spin out into the recess in the stem, leaving the pellet free to move forward; the creep spring prevents any rebound action, and also prevents the pellet from creeping forward during flight. On graze or impact, the pellet is carried forward on to the needle, firing the detonator, the magazine of the fuze, and the bursting charge of the shell.

See page 12 for notes *re* other fuzes of No. 83 type.

Fuze, Time and Percussion, No. 85.

C.I.W. Design 1,909.

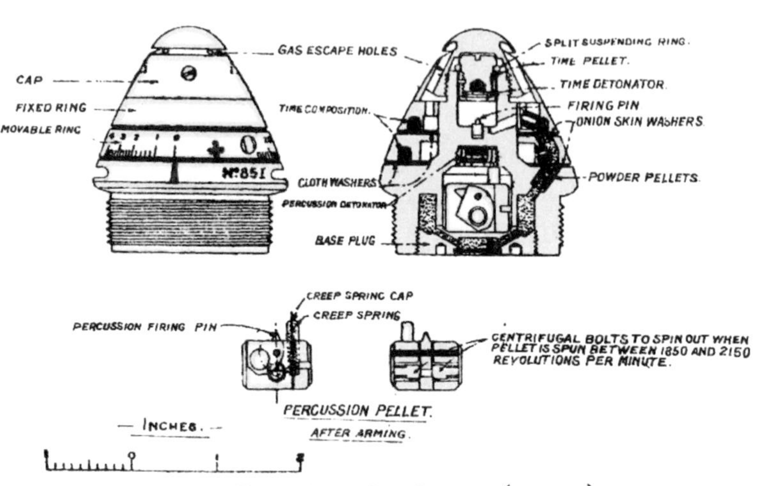

Time of burning, 23 secs. (approx.)

Action of time arrangement.—Upon shock of discharge the time detonator pellet overcomes the support of the suspending ring and the time detonator is pierced by the firing pin. The flash passes through the side hole in the stem of the body to the powder pellet and composition in the top ring ; the composition burns round until it meets the exposed powder pellet in the bottom ring, and so on to the powder pellet and magazine in the body.

The escape hole for the burning gases is through the cap and not as in the No. 80 fuze.

Action of percussion arrangement.—The percussion pin is housed in the percussion pellet and pivoted on a steel pin. It is secured in an unarmed position by two centrifugal bolts (one on each side). The pellet is enclosed in and pinned to a brass sleeve.

Upon rotation the centrifugal bolts overcome their springs and fly outwards, this allows the percussion pin to turn on its fulcrum and arm.

The pellet is fitted in front with two creep springs, each spring is covered with a brass cap protruding from the holes which house the springs. Upon impact the brass caps are telescoped into the pellet and the armed percussion pin strikes the detonator. The flash passes down through the pellet to the magazine of the fuze.

See page 12 for notes *re* other fuzes of No. 85 type.

Fuze, Time and Percussion, No. 89.

R.L. Design 22,790.

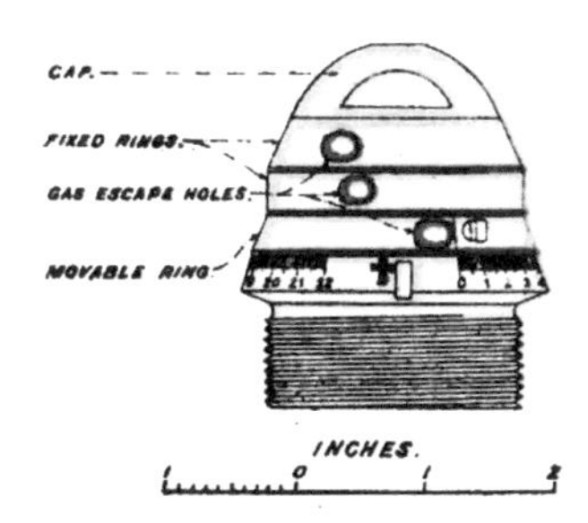

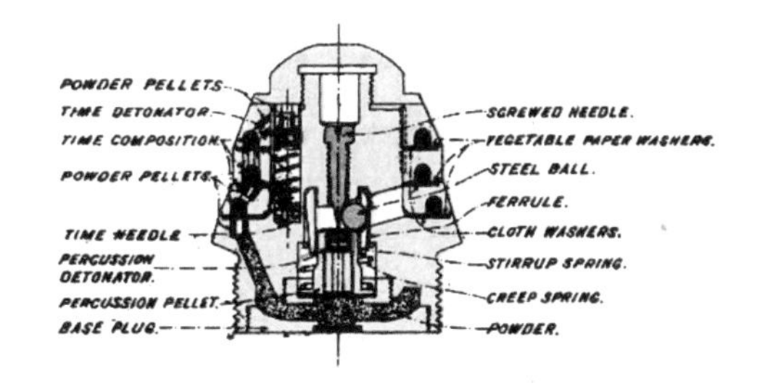

Time of burning, 60 secs. (approx.)

The action of this fuze is as follows :—

Time portion.—On shock of discharge, the time detonator pellet sets back, compresses the spiral spring, and carries the detonator on to the time needle. The flash from the detonator, reinforced by that of a powder pellet, ignites the time composition in the top ring. This burns round until it reaches a powder pellet at the beginning of the composition in the middle ring. The latter composition is then ignited and burns round in the opposite direction until it reaches an exposed powder pellet in the bottom (movable) ring, the time composition in which ignites and burns round until it reaches the flash hole leading to the magazine of the fuze. As the composition in each ring is ignited, so the brass discs which close the escape holes are blown out. It should be noted that even with the fuze set at "0" the composition in the top ring must burn completely round, before the magazine is fired. The position of the powder pellet in the bottom time ring relative to the composition channels in the top and middle rings, governs the length of composition in the middle and bottom rings which will consequently be burnt, and depends upon the setting of the fuze.

Percussion portion.—On shock of discharge, the ferrule sets back, straightening out the arms of its stirrup spring, unmasking the front of the percussion pellet, and releasing the safety ball. The rotary motion of the shell causes the ball to spin out into the recess in the stem leaving the pellet free to move forward. The creep spring prevents any rebound action and also prevents the pellet from creeping forward during flight. On graze or impact, the pellet is carried forward on to the needle, firing the detonator, the magazine of the fuze and the bursting charge of the shell.

No. 80 Type Fuzes.

Various Marks of No. 80 fuzes are in the Service, differing in the material from which they are made and their consequent construction. The action of each, however, is the same.

No. 80 B, T. & P. Fuzes are No. 80 fuzes without the lip ; i.e., they will fit into shell not provided with a recess at the nose.

No. 80/44 & 80B/44 Time Fuzes are used for time H.E. shell. They have no percussion mechanism. The graduations between 0 and 2 are blacked out as a warning not to set these fuzes between 0 and 2. Earlier issues had stop pins fitted to prevent setting between 0 and 2.

No. 87 T. & P. Fuzes have no lip and the rings are filled with composition to give 30 secs. burning (approx.)

No. 87/44 Time Fuzes are No. 87 fuzes converted on the lines of No. 80/44 fuzes.

No. 180 & 180B Time Fuzes are used for shrapnel and incendiary shell for A.A. purposes and for star shell. They are converted from No. 80 & No. 80B fuzes and have no percussion mechanism.

No. 83 Type Fuzes.

Various modifications of No. 83 fuzes have been introduced. Although No. 83 Marks III. and IV. fuzes have no time safety pin, the time mechanism arms more readily in the gun than the time mechanism of the No. 83 Mark II. fuze. No. 83 Mark II. fuzes are therefore being issued with weaker time strirrup springs to approximate to the spiral spring in the No. 83, Mark III.—IV. fuzes and such fuzes will be known as **No. 83 R.** They will have their caps painted black.

No. 88 T. & P. Fuzes are No. 83 fuzes having their lower rings filled with a slower burning composition, thus giving a total time of burning of about 45 seconds. They have their lower rings lacquered red.

No. 88R T. & P. Fuzes are No. 83R fuzes filled with slower burning composition as in No. 88 fuzes. They will have their caps painted black and lower rings lacquered red.

No. 83/44 Time Fuzes are converted from No. 83R or No. 83, Mark III—IV fuzes. They are for use in time H.E. shell. They have no percussion mechanism, the graduations between 0 and 2 are blacked out, and the fuzes have a blue "T" painted on.

No. 94 T. & P. Fuzes are No. 83R or 83, Marks III.—IV. fuzes with the time rings filled with a special long burning powder to give approximately 40 seconds burning. They are distinguishable by having the time rings lacquered blue.

No. 85 Type Fuzes.

No. 85/44 Time Fuzes are used for time H.E. shell. They have no percussion mechanism. The graduations between 0 and 2 are blacked out as a warning not to set these fuzes between 0 and 2. A blue "T" is painted on each fuze.

No. 185 Time Fuzes are used for shrapnel and incendiary shell for A.A. purposes, and for star shell. They are converted from No. 85 fuzes and have no percussion mechanism. A blue "T" is painted on each fuze.

Fuze, Percussion, Base, Hotchkiss.

R.L. Design 9,310 C, etc.

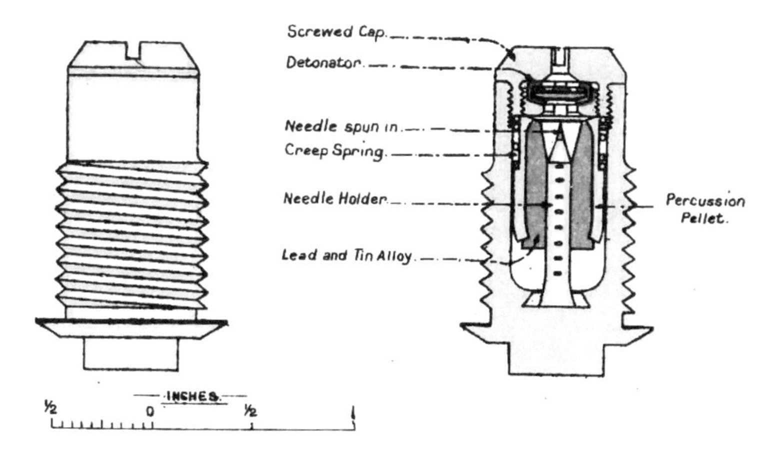

Action.—On the shock of discharge, the pellet sets back over the needle holder, thus allowing the steel needle to project beyond it. The alloy at the bottom of the pellet cushions against the bottom of the fuze, and a small portion of it dovetails into the undercut recess, round the base of the needle holder. This form a weak connection between the pellet and fuze body, and assists the spring in checking rebound action. On graze or impact, the pellet and needle set forward, the needle pierces the detonator, and the flash passes through to the bursting charge of the shell.

The Mark VI. fuze differs from the Mark IV. fuze, in as much as it is more sensitive and can be used with lower chamber pressures, and has no undercut recess at the base.

Fuze, Percussion, D.A. Impact, No. 18.

R.L. Design 13,420 E.

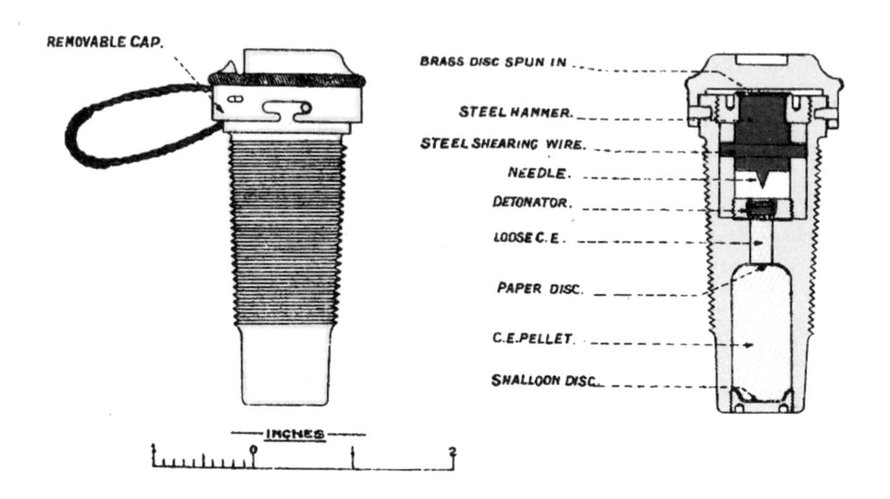

Action.—At the last moment before loading, the securing pin and safety cap are removed. The fuze is quiescent in all its parts till direct impact takes place, when the steel hammer is crushed in shearing its steel pin, and carrying its needle point on to the detonator. The explosion of the detonator fires the loose composition exploding in the central channel, which in turn fires the magazine of the fuze and the bursting charge of the shell.

Fuze, Percussion, Direct Action, with Cap, No. 44.

R.L. Designs 23,810 A and 26,620.

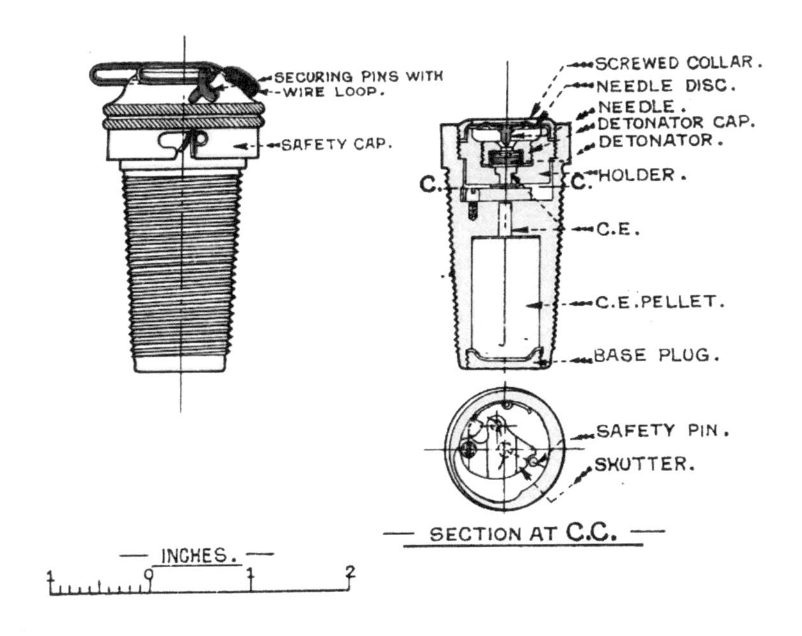

Action.—Before loading, the securing pins and safety cap are removed.

Nothing takes place on shock of discharge, but on rotation, centrifugal force causes the shutter to swing open and so bring the C.E. in the shutter in line with that below the detonator and in the channel leading to the magazine.

Upon impact, the needle disc is crushed in, carrying its needle on to the detonator, the loose C.E. below the detonator and in the shutter is fired, the diaphragm is broken and the C.E. in the magazine is detonated. The detonation of the C.E. in the magazine is transmitted to the bursting charge in the shell.

Fuze No. 44 B is similar to above, but has a weaker shutter spring to enable the fuze to be used with large guns and howitzers.

Fuze No. $\frac{44}{80}$ is similar to above, but is issued without a cap or safety pin (and usually in place in the shell) for use under a time fuze. It has a stronger shutter spring than No. 44 fuze to render the fuze safer.

Fuze No. $\frac{44}{83}$ is similar to fuze No. $\frac{44}{80}$, but has a shutter spring intermediate in strength between Nos. 44 and $\frac{44}{80}$ fuzes.

Fuze, Percussion, Direct Action, Impact, No. 45.

R.L. Designs 25,230 and 27,060.

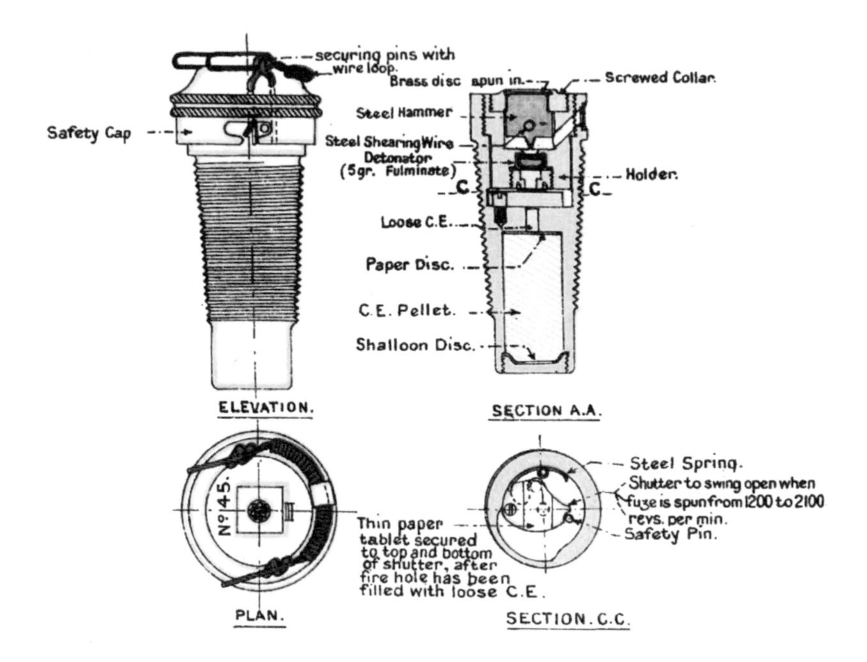

Action.—Before loading, the securing pins and safety cap are removed.

Nothing takes place on shock of discharge, but on rotation, centrifugal force causes the shutter to swing open and so bring the C.E. in the shutter in line with that below the detonator and in the channel leading to the magazine.

Upon impact, the steel hammer is driven in, shears the shearing wire and fires the detonator. The loose C.E. below the detonator and in the shutter is fired, the diaphragm is broken, and the C.E in the magazine is detonated. The detonation of the C.E. in the magazine is transmitted to the bursting charge in the shell.

Fuzes, Percn., Nos. 101, 102 & 103, with Gaine No. 2.

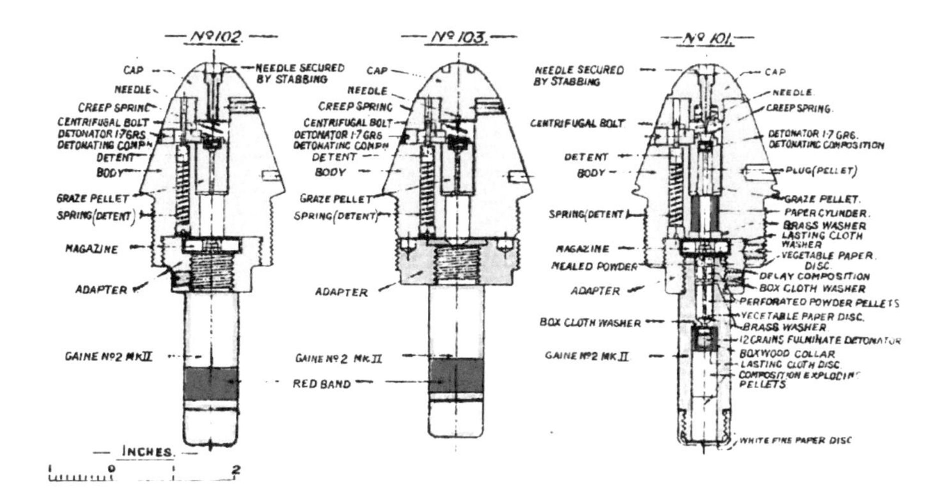

Action.—On firing, the detent sets back, compressing its spring. When the upper end of the pin is clear of the fuze body, centrifugal force carries it over, and the spring, re-asserting itself, jambs the pin under the shoulder of the recess. The withdrawal of the detent allows the centrifugal bolt to come out and so free the graze pellet. On graze or impact the graze pellet moves forward on to the needle and the flash from the detonator passes through the centre of the pellet to the magazine and gaine.

Magazine.—Fuzes Nos. 101 and 102 were fitted with a magazine formed from two tin cups, one telescoping within the other, and having a central brass fitment. The fitment carried a powder pellet **with** or **without** delay. The annulus of the magazine was filled with powder.

Gaine.—The gaine, made up as shewn is fitted **with** and **without** delay. The upper copper shell being filled with a powder pellet, or delay composition and a shorter powder pellet as shewn.

Shutter.—A shutter has now been introduced into fuze No. 101. It fits into the adapter in place of magazine and only opens to allow the flash from the detonator to reach the gaine when the shell is rotating. When so fitted, the fuze is known as 101E. The adapter under No. 103 fuze is also fitted with a shutter similar to that in No. 101E fuze.

For latest No. 101E fuze and gaine, and notes re other fuzes of No. 100 type see page 18.

Fuze, Perc., No. 101 E, and Gaine No. 2, with delay.

Design R.L. 25,360 (Fuze) and R.L. 23,676 (Gaine), etc.

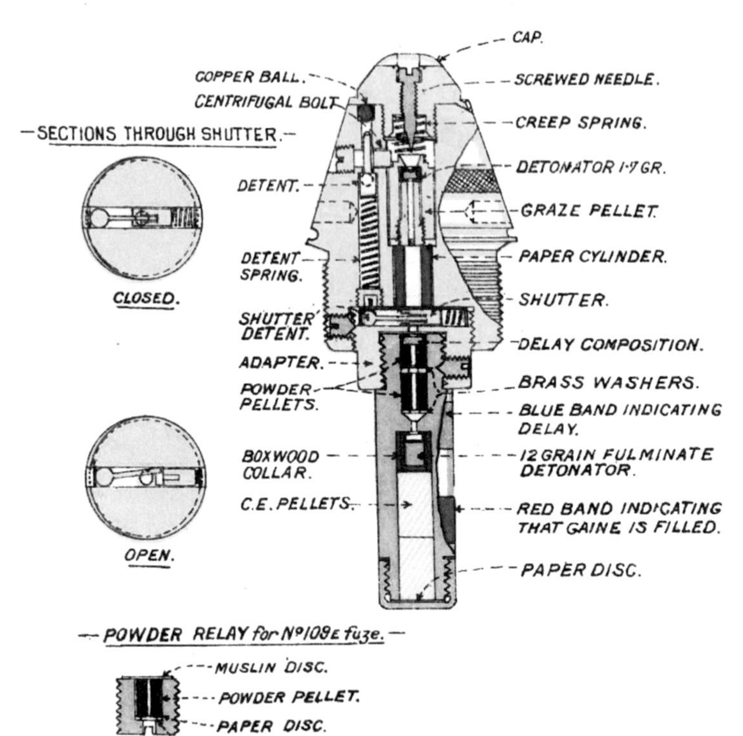

For description and action of this fuze see page 17.

No. 100 Type Fuzes.

No. 100 Fuze was the first fuze of this series. It was introduced as a graze action fuze, with a cocked cross pellet carrying a detonator for sensitive graze action. This fuze carried a No. 1 gaine (*i.e.*, long pattern), but all gaines now fitted are No. 2 (*i.e.*, short pattern).

No. 101 Fuze is No. 100 fuze without the cross pellet, the detonator being inserted in the graze pellet. When fitted with a shutter, this fuze becomes **No. 101 E.** When fitted with a stronger creep spring for use in 6-inch gun, the fuze becomes **No. 101 EX** (or **No. 101 XE).** For use in larger howitzers, the fuze is fitted with weaker detent and shutter springs and is then known as **No. 101 B.** All these fuzes carry a gaine.

No. 102 Fuze is chiefly converted from fuze No. 100, and is generally the same as No. 101 fuze. This fuze carries a gaine.

No. 103 Fuze is similar to No. 101 fuze, but has the lower end of the fuze cut short. It does not carry a gaine itself, but is screwed into shell over an adapter which carries the gaine.

No. 108 Fuze is No. 100 fuze without a gaine, used for shell filled powder.

No. 109 Fuze is No. 101 or No. 102 fuze without a gaine, with adapter plugged, and used for shell filled powder and chemical shell.

No. 109E Fuze is similar to No. 109 fuze, but has a shutter similar to No. 101E fuze. It does not carry a gaine, but the adapter plug used in No. 109 fuze is replaced by a powder relay (see illustration above.) This fuze is used in powder filled shell and chemical shell.

Fuze, Percussion, with Cap, No. 106, Mark III.

I.D.W. Design 3853.

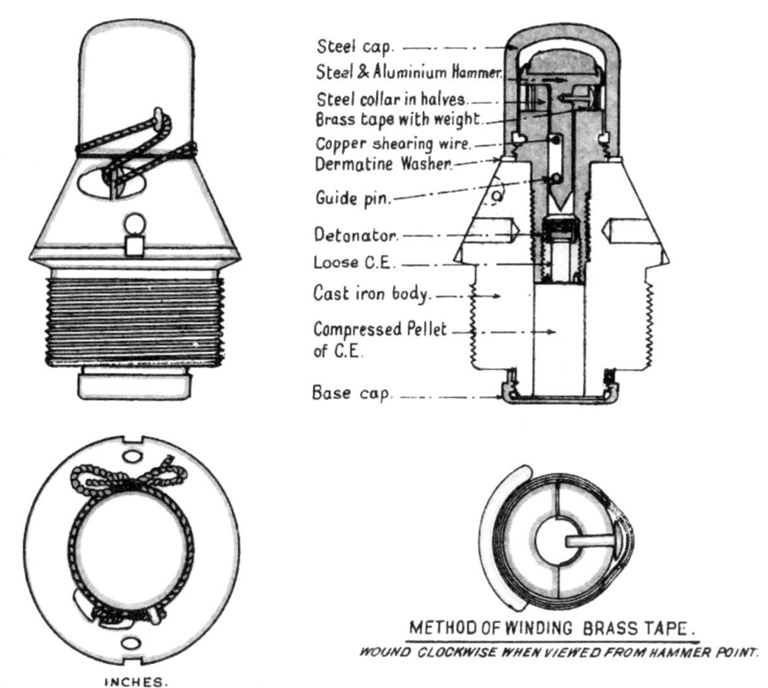

Description.—The body of fuze is drilled on its axis to contain at its lower end a pellet of H.E., above this a brass plug carrying a detonator, and again above this a spindle having a needle point immediately above the detonator and a head at its upper end. The hammer head, spindle and needle is prevented from moving back on to the detonator on firing by a steel split collar, which fits between the underside of the hammer head and the top face of the steel bush screwed into the fuze body.

To retain this split steel collar in position a brass tape is wound round it three times.

Action.—When the shell leaves the gun the effect of centrifugal force causes the tape to become unwound, this releasing the split collar.

The hammer is now only prevented from being pushed back on to the detonator by the shearing wire, which passes through a slot in the hammer spindle.

On striking, this wire is sheared and the needle at the lower end of the hammer spindle driven into the detonator.

For the dual purpose of preventing damage to the hammer head if a shell were dropped accidentally and for excluding moisture, the whole top of the fuze is provided with a steel cap which makes an air-tight joint when screwed down on to the dermatine washer. The cap is prevented from coming unscrewed by a becket which is tied between the eyes on the body and cap respectively.

Fuze, Percussion, with Cap, No. 106 E.

R.L. Design 26,600.

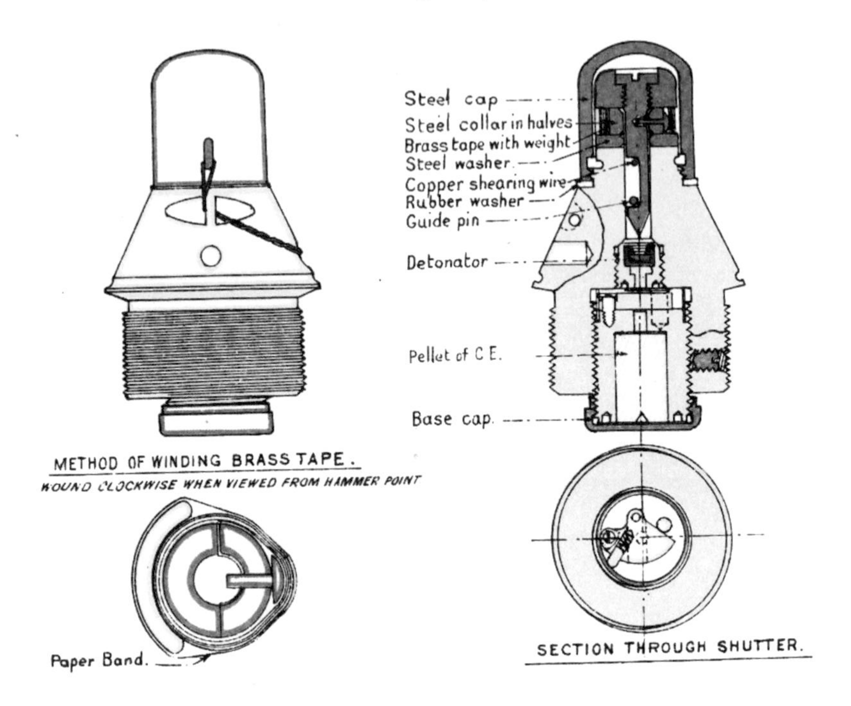

Description.—This fuze is similar to that described on page 19 but the lower portion is filled with a bush which carries a shutter on its upper face to render the fuze safe from premature action on rough usage or in the gun.

Action.—The action of this fuze is similar to that on the preceding page, except that the shutter remains closed while the projectile is travelling up the bore. The shutter then opens and brings the hole filled with C.E. in the shutter over the channel in the bush leading to the C.E. pellet, a thin diaphragm separating the C.E. in the shutter from the C.E. in the channel below. On impact, the detonator fires the C.E. in the shutter which breaks through the diaphragm and detonates the C.E. in the channel and the pellet below. This fuze has, therefore, a similarity with fuze No. 44 described on page 15.

Notes on the Marking of Shells, Cartridges and Fuzes and their Packages.

The following marking and stencilling of ammunition was adopted on consignments issued after September, 1916,* the abbreviations, markings, and stencillings used being :—

General :

A.A.	for Anti-Aircraft
A.Z.	for Anti-Zeppelin
Ammn.	for Ammunition
Bal.	for Ballistite
B.L., Q.F.	omitted unless there is a B.L. and Q.F. gun of the same calibre
C.E.	for Composition Exploding
C.S.P.	for Chilworth Smokeless Powder
Cartges.	for Cartridges
Chem.	for Chemical
Cordite	for Cordite Mk. I.
Dr.	for Dram
Elec.	for Electric
Expr.	for Exploder
Fuzed	retained in full
G.	for Gaine
G.2.	for Gaine, No. 2
Gun	where necessary
H.	for Heavy
H.E.	for High Explosive
How.	for Howitzer
Imp.	for Impulse
Incdy.	for Incendiary
L.	for Light
Lot	retained when referring to propellants and fuzes
M.D.	for Cordite M.D.
Mk.	for Mark
N.C.T.	for Nitrocellulose
P.P.	for Picric Powder
Perc.	for Percussion
Phos.	for Phosphorus.
Pr.	for Pounder
Shrap.	for Shrapnel
" Size "	this word is now omitted when referring to propellants
T. & P.	for Time and Percussion
T.N.T.	for Trotyl
"	for Inch

* For modifications to these abbreviations, markings and stencillings introduced in the latter part of 1917 see pages miscellaneous, 4–10.

TIPS, BANDS, ETC., ON SHELL.

TIPS.

Old Marking. (*Prior to Sept.*, 1916)	*Marking.* (*Sept.*, 1916)	*Signification*
White	White	Shot
Red	Red	Shrapnel
—	Black	Absence of smoke producer in Amatol of H.E. shells

RINGS (round nose of shell).

White	—	Steel except star and shrapnel
White (two)	White (two)	Armour piercing
Red	Red	Filled
Green	—	Trotyl exploders
—	Black	For H.E. shell requiring powder-filled fuzes

In the case of Incendiary Shell without H.E. filling, a one inch black band was painted round the nose of the shell, over which a half inch red ring was painted, to indicate that the shell was filled.

BANDS (round body of shell).

Green	Green	Trotyl or Amatol
Red	Red (round gaine)	C.E.
Blue	Blue (round gaine)	Delay
Red and White ½-inch apart	Omit	Chemical shell filled S.K. (various red and white bands to distinguish different chemicals other than S.K. substituted).

Coloured bands on shells carried in slings were 3-inches above the centre so as not to be obscured.

BODY PAINTING.

Old Method. (*Prior to Sept.*, 1916).	*Method* (*Sept.*, 1916).	*Signification.*
Black	Black	Filled black powder
Yellow	Yellow	„ H.E.
Yellow	Grey	„ chemical
—	Red	Incendiary
Yellow—point to shoulder Red—shoulder to base	Yellow—point to shoulder Red—shoulder to base	Incendiary with H.E. filling.

MARKS.

Star	Star	Star shell
⊕ three times.	⊕ once.	To indicate position of C. of G. in shell 12-in. and upwards.

FUZES.

Blue disc	Blue disc	Delay (marked on boxes)
Blue tip	Blue tip	Delay
Green tip	Green tip	Tested needles
Red and black	—	No. 44 modifications
Blue T	Blue T	A.A. purposes

Black Tip :—

As the majority of H.E. shell had a smoke box or smoke bag included in their filling, it was decided to mark those not so filled, rather than *vice versa.*

Green or Black Ring :—

The use of a black ring on H.E. shells which denoted the necessity for a powder filled fuze, served the same purpose as the previous green ring, denoting unsuitability for such fuzes. The green ring was therefore dropped.

Red Ring :—

In the case of H.E. shell suitable for issue to hot climates, the red ring was broken up into a ring of crosses.

Weight :—

This was stencilled on the shoulder for better preservation.

Shells 4·5-in. and upwards, above the normal weight, were marked with three discs. Shells between the normal weight and 0·5 per cent. below were marked with two discs. Shells between 0·5 per cent. below and 1 per cent. below were marked with one disc. When more than 1 per cent. below the normal weight, the actual filled weight was stencilled on the shell. Weight markings were omitted on Shrapnel and practice shot which are accurately adjusted to weight and should never require anything except two discs.

Initials of Filling Factory and date of Filling .—

Stencilling of this marking was retained and the initials and date of filling were stamped in small lettering.

Calibre and Numeral :—

Not shewn on shells of fixed ammunition, but both were given on other shell.

Design No. of Filling :—

This was stencilled on all shell (except Shrapnel and powder filled) and this obviated stencilling of such symbols as ▐▌▐▌ ■ or words **"Block," "Exploder Container,"** etc.

Certain details of filling were however, stencilled, such as the number and weight of exploders, and tracer markings.

Centre of Gravity :—

Stencilled in one place only instead of three.

Filled Weight Markings on H.E. Shell.

Up till recently the weight markings on H.E. Shell has been given as follows :—

Symbol.	Significance.	Application.
Three discs ⁖	Above mean weight to + ½ %	9·2-in. shell & below
Two discs ..	Mean weight to − ½ % inclusive	Do.
One disc .	Between − ½ % and − 1 %	Do.

(Discs black, 1-in. dia.)

Actual Weight.

(*a*)	To nearest ½ lb. (3·7-in. to 6-in.) To nearest 1 lb. (8-in. and 9·2-in.)	(*a*) 9·2-in. and below. outside disc limits.
(*b*)	To nearest 1 lb.	(*b*) All 12-in. & above.

(The **Weight Marking on H.E. Shell** is now being given as in the table on page, miscellaneous, 9).

General Notes on Shell Markings.

(Introduced at end of 1917).

BODY COLOURING.

Colour.	Nature of Shell.
Yellow.	High Explosive.
Black.	Shrapnel, Star, Steel shell, Common Pointed shell.
*Light Grey.	Chemical.
*Light Green.	Smoke (Phosphorus).
*Red.	Incendiary.

* These colours are also painted on packages containing the shell.

TIPS.

Colour	Shell.
Black.	Shell filled amatol when smoke mixture is omitted.
Red.	Shrapnel Shell.

COLOURED BANDS OR RINGS.

Colour.	Position.	Significance.	Shell.
Green.	*a.* on body.	H.E. filling other than lyddite.	Boxed, including fixed ammunition
	b. above shoulder	,,	Other than boxed ammunition.
Red.	On nose.	Filled shell.	All except Incdy.
Light Brown.	On nose, below red ring.	Cast Iron shell.	

Red crosses.	On nose instead of red ring.	Suitable for use in hot climates.	Amatol filled.
Black.	Immediately in front of driving band.	Shell suitable for use in gun.	All gun shell where gun & How. of same calibre exist.
2 White.	On nose, above & below red ring.	Armour piercing.	A.P. shell.
Various. (see table on page Chemical 1.)	On body.	Nature of filling.	Chemical shell.
Yellow.	On body.	For practice.	All practice projectiles.

Miscellaneous.

1. *Exploder marking* is only provided when C.E. exploders are used.

2. 80/20 is not stencilled on shell so filled, but shell filled trotyl will have "TROTYL" in $\frac{3}{4}$-in. letters on the green band.

3. Shell so manufactured or filled that only one type of fuze *can* be used have "USE.........FUZE" stencilled above the green band.

Diagrams of Marking and Stencilling on Shell.

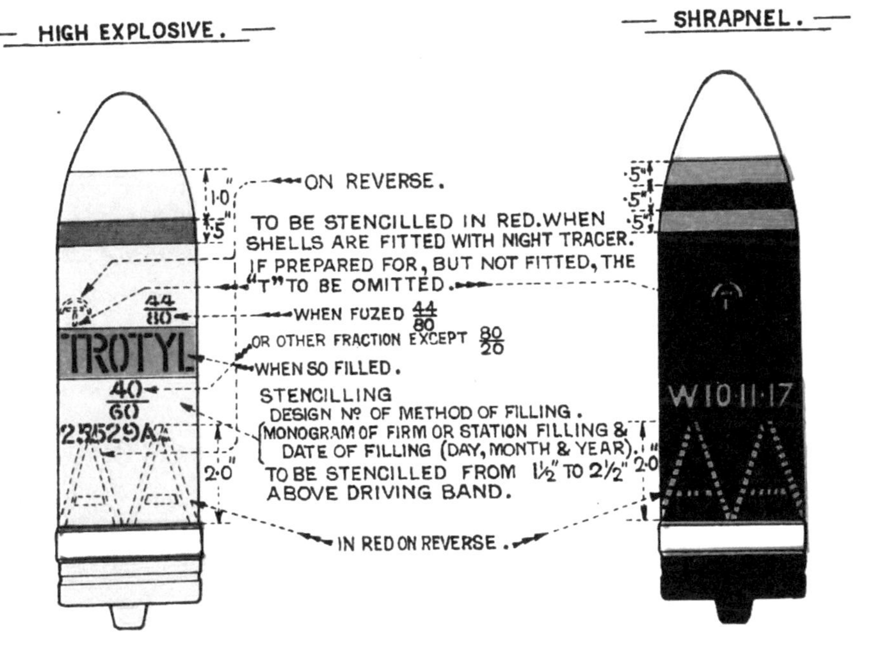

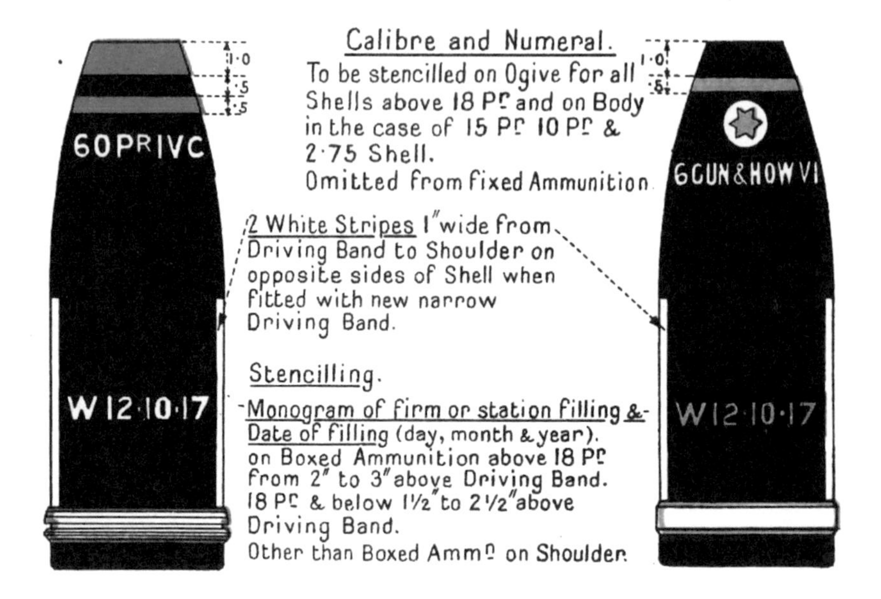
SHRAPNEL
STAR
Calibre and Numeral.
To be stencilled on Ogive for all Shells above 18 Pr. and on Body in the case of 15 Pr. 10 Pr. & 2·75 Shell.
Omitted from fixed Ammunition
1·0
·5
60 PR IVC
6 GUN & HOW VI
2 White Stripes 1" wide from Driving Band to Shoulder on opposite sides of Shell when fitted with new narrow Driving Band.
Stencilling.
Monogram of firm or station filling & Date of filling (day, month & year).
on Boxed Ammunition above 18 Pr. from 2" to 3" above Driving Band.
18 Pr. & below 1½" to 2½" above Driving Band.
Other than Boxed Ammn. on Shoulder.
W 12·10·17

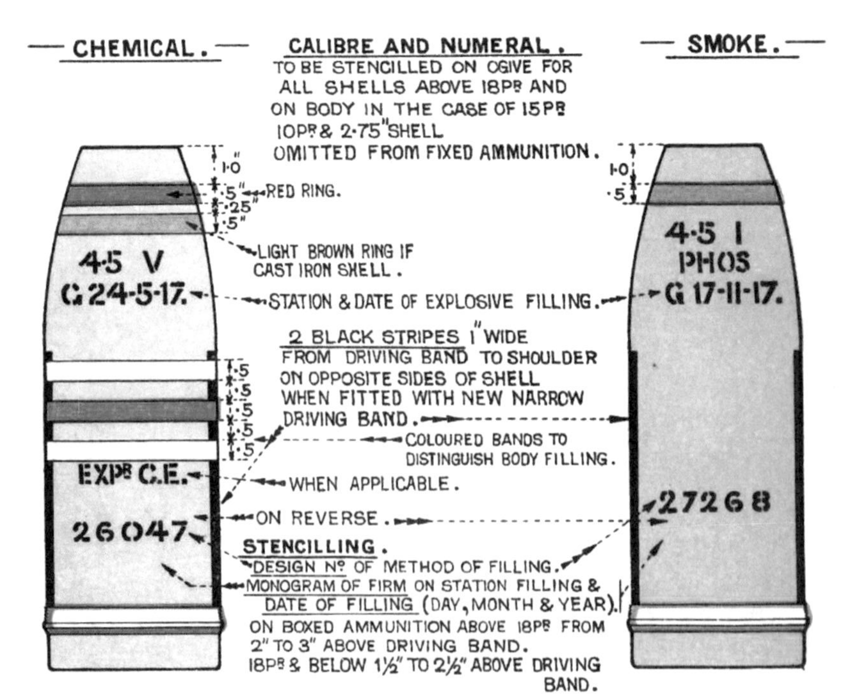
CHEMICAL.
CALIBRE AND NUMERAL.
SMOKE.
TO BE STENCILLED ON OGIVE FOR ALL SHELLS ABOVE 18PR AND ON BODY IN THE CASE OF 15PR 10PR & 2·75" SHELL
OMITTED FROM FIXED AMMUNITION.
1·0"
·5"
·25"
RED RING.
LIGHT BROWN RING IF CAST IRON SHELL.
4·5 V
G 24-5-17.
4·5 I
PHOS
G 17-11-17.
STATION & DATE OF EXPLOSIVE FILLING.
2 BLACK STRIPES 1" WIDE FROM DRIVING BAND TO SHOULDER ON OPPOSITE SIDES OF SHELL WHEN FITTED WITH NEW NARROW DRIVING BAND.
COLOURED BANDS TO DISTINGUISH BODY FILLING.
EXPR C.E.
WHEN APPLICABLE.
26047
27268
ON REVERSE.
STENCILLING.
DESIGN No. OF METHOD OF FILLING.
MONOGRAM OF FIRM ON STATION FILLING & DATE OF FILLING (DAY, MONTH & YEAR).
ON BOXED AMMUNITION ABOVE 18PR FROM 2" TO 3" ABOVE DRIVING BAND.
18PR & BELOW 1½" TO 2½" ABOVE DRIVING BAND.

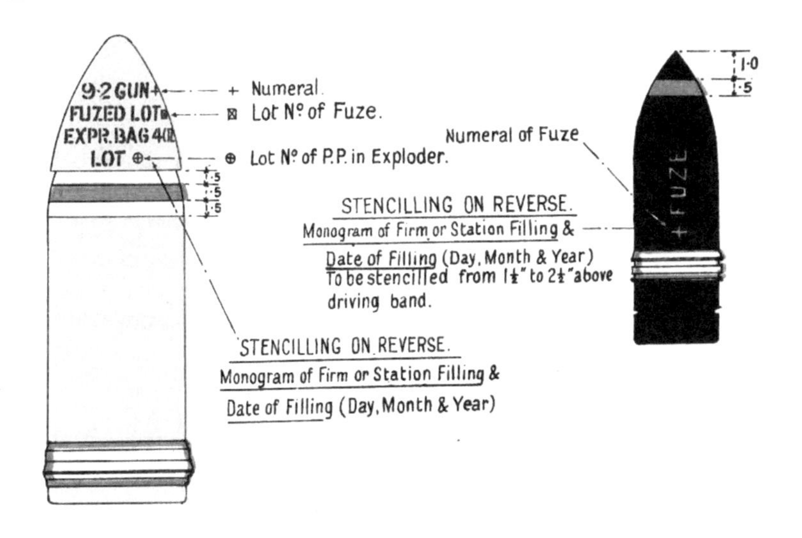
9·2 A.P. WITH CAP.
9·2 GUN
FUZED LOT
EXPR. BAG
LOT
+ Numeral.
⊠ Lot Nº of Fuze.
⊕ Lot Nº of P.P. in Exploder.
·5
·5
·5
STENCILLING ON REVERSE.
Monogram of Firm or Station Filling &
Date of Filling (Day, Month & Year)
6 PR STEEL SHELL.
1·0
·5
Numeral of Fuze
FUZE
STENCILLING ON REVERSE.
Monogram of Firm or Station Filling &
Date of Filling (Day, Month & Year)
To be stencilled from 1¼" to 2¼" above driving band.

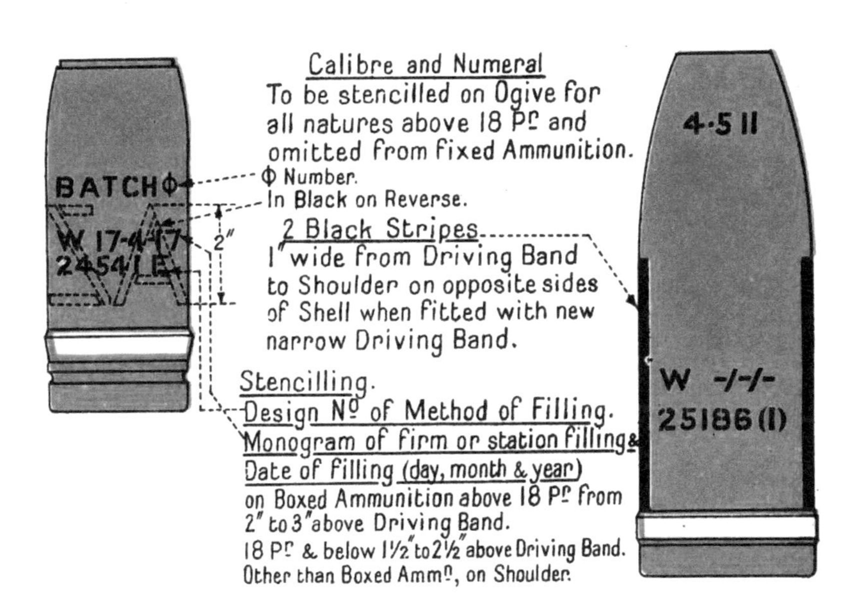
INCENDIARY.
3-INCH.
BATCH
W 17-4-17
2454 LE
2"
Calibre and Numeral
To be stencilled on Ogive for all natures above 18 Pr and omitted from fixed Ammunition.
Φ Number.
In Black on Reverse.
2 Black Stripes
1" wide from Driving Band to Shoulder on opposite sides of Shell when fitted with new narrow Driving Band.
Stencilling.
Design Nº of Method of Filling.
Monogram of firm or station filling &
Date of filling (day, month & year)
on Boxed Ammunition above 18 Pr from 2" to 3" above Driving Band.
18 Pr & below 1½" to 2½" above Driving Band.
Other than Boxed Ammn, on Shoulder.
4·5 II
W -/-/-
25186 (I)

High Explosive.

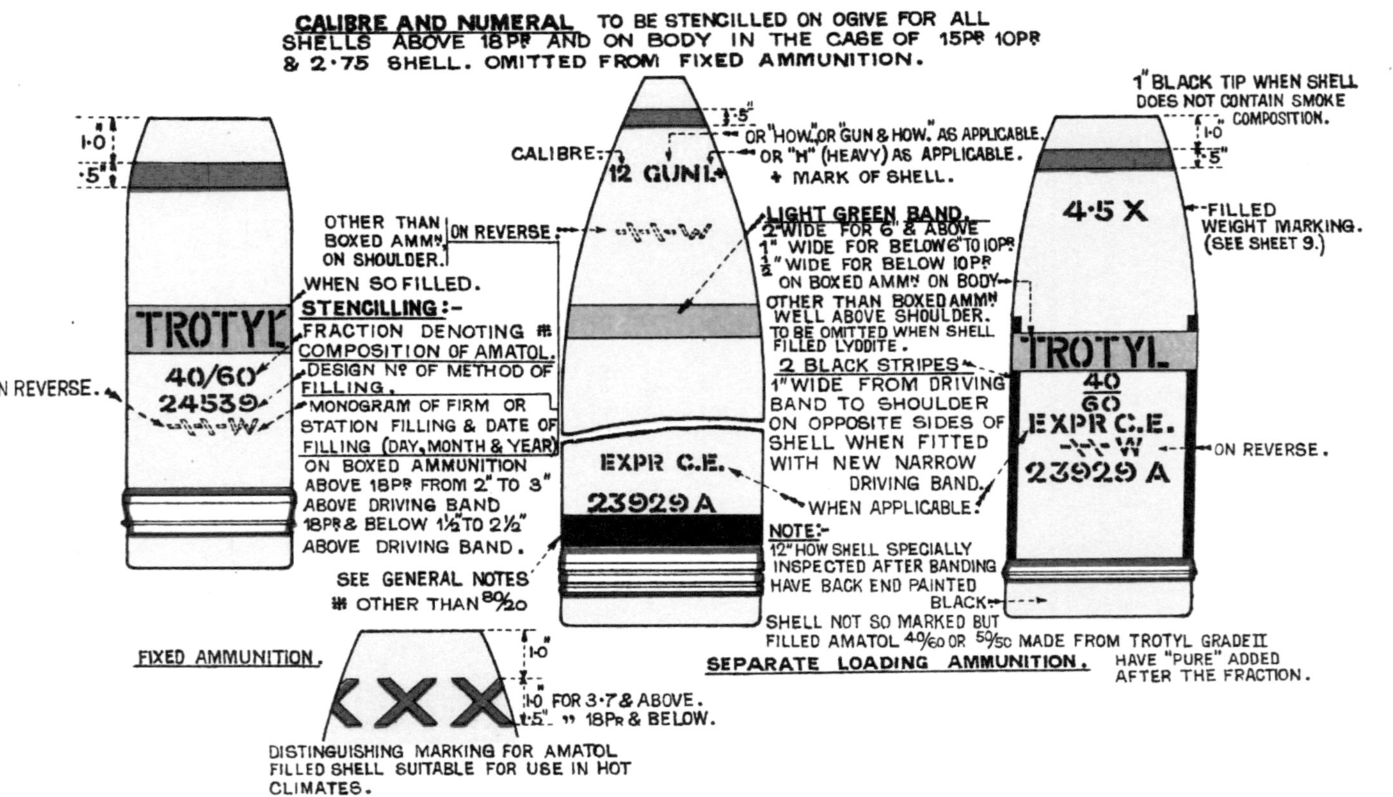

WEIGHT MARKING ON FILLED H.E., SMOKE, CHEMICAL AND INCENDIARY SHELL.

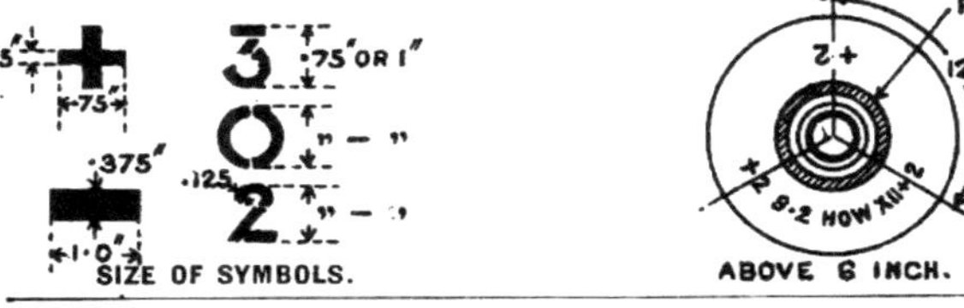

ON SEPARATE LOADING AMMUNITION, stencilling is placed on the nose of the shell in line with the calibre and numeral ; in 3 equidistant spaces for shell above 6-in., and in 2 places for shell 6-in. to 3·7-in. inclusive.

ON FIXED AMMUNITION the marking is placed half-way up the ogive.

TABLE OF WEIGHTS.

For ± 3 units on each calibre of H.E. Shell, 3·7-in. to 15-in.

The weights in any square are inclusive, the words "above" and "below" applying throughout the respective lines.

UNIT.	¼-LB.			½-LB.			1-LB.		2-LB.				5-LB.		10-LB.	
CAL.	3·7-IN.	4-IN.	4·5-IN.	4·7-IN.	60 PR.	5-IN.	6-IN.	7·5-IN.	8-IN.	9·2-IN. How.	9·2-IN. Gun.	10-IN.	12-IN. Gun.	12-IN. How.	14-IN. Heavy	15-IN. How.
SYMBOL.	lb. oz.	lb. oz.	lb. oz.	lb. oz.	lb. oz.	lb. oz.	lb. oz.	lb. oz.	lb. oz.	lb. oz.	lb. oz.	lb. oz.	lb. oz.	lb. oz.	lb. oz.	lb. oz.
+3	20 14	31 14	35 14	46 12	61 12	41 12	103 8	203 8	207 0	297 0	387 0	507 0	867 8	767 8	1621 0	1435 0
	above 20 10	31 10	35 10	46 4	61 4	41 4	102 8	202 8	205 0	295 0	385 0	505 0	862 8	762 8	1611 0	1425 0
+2	20 10	31 10	35 10	46 4	61 4	41 4	102 8	202 8	205 0	295 0	385 0	505 0	862 8	762 8	1611 0	1425 0
	above 20 6	31 6	35 6	45 12	60 12	40 12	101 8	201 8	203 0	293 0	383 0	503 0	857 8	757 8	1601 0	1415 0
+1	20 6	31 6	35 6	45 12	60 12	40 12	101 8	201 8	203 0	293 0	383 0	503 0	857 8	757 8	1601 0	1415 0
	above 20 2	31 2	35 2	45 4	60 4	40 4	100 8	200 8	201 0	291 0	381 0	501 0	852 8	752 8	1591 0	1405 0
0	20 2	31 2	35 2	45 4	60 4	40 4	100 8	200 8	201 0	291 0	381 0	501 0	852 8	752 8	1591 0	1405 0
	19 14	30 14	34 14	44 12	59 12	39 12	99 8	199 8	199 0	289 0	379 0	499 0	847 8	747 8	1581 0	1395 9
−1	below 19 14	30 14	34 14	44 12	59 12	39 12	99 8	199 8	199 0	289 0	379 0	499 0	847 8	747 8	1581 0	1395 0
	19 10	30 10	34 10	44 4	59 4	39 4	98 8	198 8	197 0	287 0	377 0	497 0	842 8	742 8	1571 0	1385 0
−2	below 19 10	30 10	34 10	44 4	59 4	39 4	98 8	198 8	197 0	287 0	377 0	497 0	842 8	742 8	1571 0	1385 0
	19 6	30 6	34 6	43 12	58 12	38 12	97 8	197 8	195 0	285 0	375 0	495 0	837 8	737 8	1561 0	1375 0
−3	below 19 6	30 6	34 6	43 12	58 12	38 12	97 8	197 8	195 0	285 0	375 0	495 0	837 8	737 8	1561 0	1375 0
	19 2	30 2	34 2	43 4	58 4	38 4	96 8	196 8	193 0	283 0	373 0	493 0	832 8	732 8	1551 0	1365 0

WEIGHTS OF FUZES, PLUGS, ADAPTERS, ETC.

	lb.	oz.		lb.	oz.		lb.	oz.
Fuze No. 101 and Gaine	2	10¼	Adapter Fuze Hole No. 2, Mark II. ...	1	0¾	Plug Fuze Hole, 2-in., No. 3, Mark V....	1	12½
Fuze No. 44		8¼	Plug Fuze Hole, Special, No. 1, Mark III.		8¼	Plug Fuze Hole, 2-in., No. 8, Mark III.	2	6

The filled weight of the shell is the weight filled and fuzed.

(A.) With No. 101 Fuze and Gaine in the case of shell with 2-in. fuze hole, issued plugged.

(B.) With No. 44 Fuze in the case of shell with a G.S. fuze hole issued plugged.

(C) As issued, if issued fuzed.

If a Tracer is fitted, its weight is included in the filled weight

Method of Filling H.E. Shell, 3·7-inch and above.

The design Nos. quoted are stencilled on the shell above the driving band.

EXPLODER CONTAINER DESIGNS.

Poured Amatol.			80/20 Amatol.		
Design No.	**Particulars of Filling.**	**Calibres.**	**Design No.**	**Particulars of Filling.**	**Calibres.**
R.L. 27,222	With trotyl surround & No. 4 smoke mixture. R L. 23894A renumbered	3·7-in. and above.	R.L 23894A	COLD PRESSED. Drawing R.L. 23,894B. with "A" suffix in lieu of "B." With trotyl surround, and No. 4 smoke mixture.	4·5-in. to 10-in
R.L. 27,222 A	No trotyl surround and No. 4 smoke mixture. R.L. 23929B renumbered		R.L. 23894B	COLD PRESSED. Same design as R.L. 23,894A. but with No. 5 smoke mixture.	
			R.L. 23894C	HOT MIXED. Same design as R.L. 23,894A. but with No. 7 smoke mixture.	
			R.L. 23894D	COLD PRESSED. with long trotyl column & No. 4 smoke mixture Design R.L. 25,844 (1) renumbered.	12-in. and above.
			R.L 23894E	COLD PRESSED. Same design as 23,894D but with No. 5 smoke mixture.	
			R.L. 23894F	HOT MIXED. Same design as 23,894D but with No. 7 smoke mixture.	
			R.L. 25844D	HOT MIXED. (Originally 25844A with No. 4 smoke mixture.) Alternative design to R.L. 23,894F Has 50/50 amatol topping in lieu of long trotyl column, and provides for the use of No. 7 smoke mixture.	

NON-EXPLODER CONTAINER DESIGNS.

Poured Amatol or Trotyl or Lyddite.			80/20 Amatol.		
Design No.	**Particulars of Filling**	**Calibres.**	**Design No.**	**Particulars of Filling.**	**Calibres.**
R.L. 23929A	No trotyl surround. Filled amatol (poured) or trotyl.*	3·7-in. to 10-in.	R.L. 23865A	COLD PRESSED. Trotyl surround and No. 4 smoke mixture. R.L. 25,812 renumbered.	4·5-in. to 10-in.
	do. do. Filled lyddite.	3·7-in. and above.	R.L. 23865B	COLD PRESSED. Same design as R.L. 23,865A but with No. 5 smoke mixture.	
R.L. 23,929C	With trotyl surround. Filled amatol (poured) or trotyl.*	12-in. and above.	R.L. 23865C	HOT MIXED. Same design as R.L. 23,865A. but with No. 7 smoke mixture.	
			R.L. 23798A	COLD PRESSED. No trotyl surround & No. 4 smoke mixture. R.L. 25,811 renumbered.	3·7-in. How. only.
			R.L. 23798B	COLD PRESSED. Same design as R.L. 23,798A. but with No. 5 smoke mixture.	
	* No. 4 smoke mixture used when filled Amatol.		R L. 23798C	HOT MIXED. Same design as R.L. 23,798A. but with No. 7 smoke mixture.	

Fuzes for H.E. Shell, Present Allocation.

Nature.	Fuze No.	Percentage.
13-pr.	103	30% delay, 70 % no delay.
18-pr.	106 101 type (delay)	65% 35%
2·75-in.	103	30% delay, 70 % no delay
10-pr.	103	,, ,, ,, ,,
3·7-in. How.	103 type (no delay) 106	25% 75%
4·5-in. How.	106 101 type (no delay)	65% 35%
60-pr.	106 101 type (delay)	65% 35%
6-in. How.	106 101 type (delay)	65% 35%
6-in. Gun	106 44	65% 35%
8-in. How.	106 101 type (delay)	60% 40%
9·2-in. How.	106 101 type (delay)	60% 40%
9·2-in. Gun	106 44	30% 70%
12-in. How.	106 101 type (delay)	30% 70%
12-in. Gun	106 44	30% 70%
15-in How.	106 101 type (delay)	30% 70%

Fuzes for Shrapnel Shell.

Nature.	Fuze No.	Remarks.
10-pr.	80, T. & P.	
2·75-in.	Do.	
13-pr.	80 or 85, T. & P.	
2·95-in.	80, T. & P.	
15-pr.	Do.	
13-pr. 9 cwt.	180 or 180B, T.	A.A.
12-pr. 12 cwt.	Do.	A.A.
3-in. 20 cwt.	180 or 185, T.	A.A.
18-pr.	80 or 85, T. & P.	
18-pr.	180 or 180B, T.	A.A.
3·7-in.	82, T. & P.	
4·5-in.	Do.	
60-pr.	88 or 89, T. & P. 83R or 83 III.–IV. T. & P.	For long range.
6-in. How.	82, T. & P.	
6-in. Gun	88 or 89, T. & P.	
9·2-in. Gun	Do.	
12-in. Gun	Do.	

Fuzes for Chemical and Smoke Shell.

Nature.	Fuze No.	Remarks.
18-pr. Chemical	106	
18-pr. Smoke	106	
4·5-in. Chemical	106	
4·5-in. Smoke	44	
60-pr. Chemical	106	
6-in. How. Chemical	106	

Fuzes for Star Shell.

(New Pattern with Parachute).

Nature.	Fuze Time No.	Remarks.
2·75-in.	183	In each case, No. 183 fuze is to be the No. 83R, or 83 Mark III.–IV., T. & P. fuze without percn. mechanism.
10-pr.	183	
15-pr. B.L.	180	
13-pr.	180 or 183	
18-pr.	180	
3-in. 20 cwt.	185	
3·7-in.	183	
4·5-in.	T. & P. 82	
4·7-in.	183	
6-in. Gun and How.	183	

Method of Filling Shell, H.E., 3·7-in. and above.

R.L. Design 23,929 A.

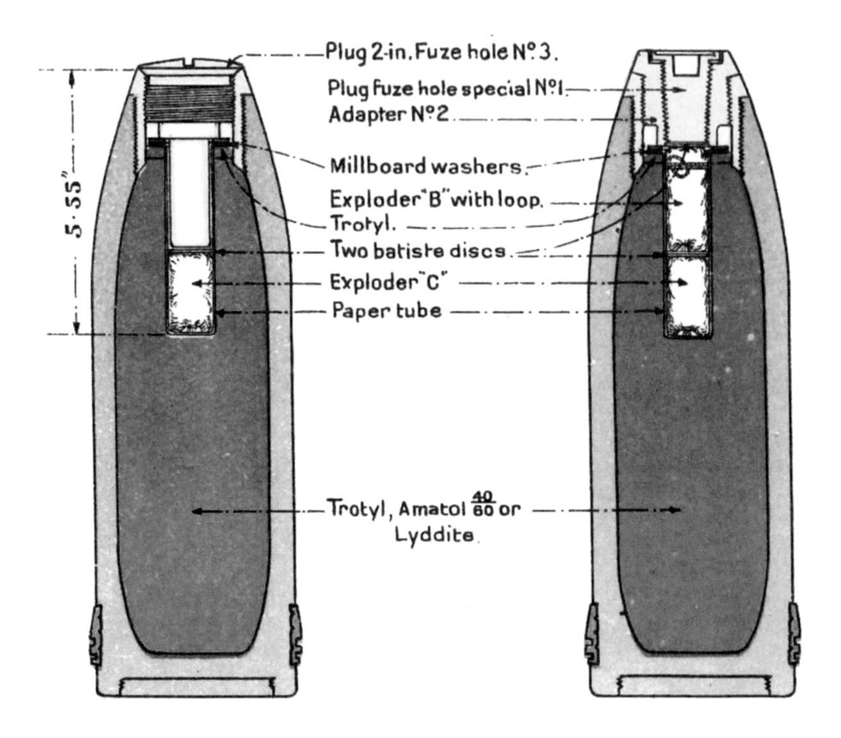

The figures above shew a 4·5-in. Howitzer shell filled $\frac{40}{60}$ amatol, trotyl or lyddite.

The explosive is poured into the shell in a molten state ; a "former," enveloped in a paper tube, is then inserted and allowed to remain until solidification takes place. The " former " is then withdrawn, leaving a paper lined cavity. The level of the filling is then adjusted by pouring trotyl as required, and completed with millboard washers.

An exploder is then placed in the cavity, compressed into place and the fuze and gaine or 2-in. fuze hole plug screwed in. If a 44 or 106 fuze is used, a further exploder is placed on top of the lower exploder and the fuze hole closed with an adapter and G.S. plug.

Method of Filling Shell, H.E., 4·5-in. and above.

R.L. Design 23,865 A—C.

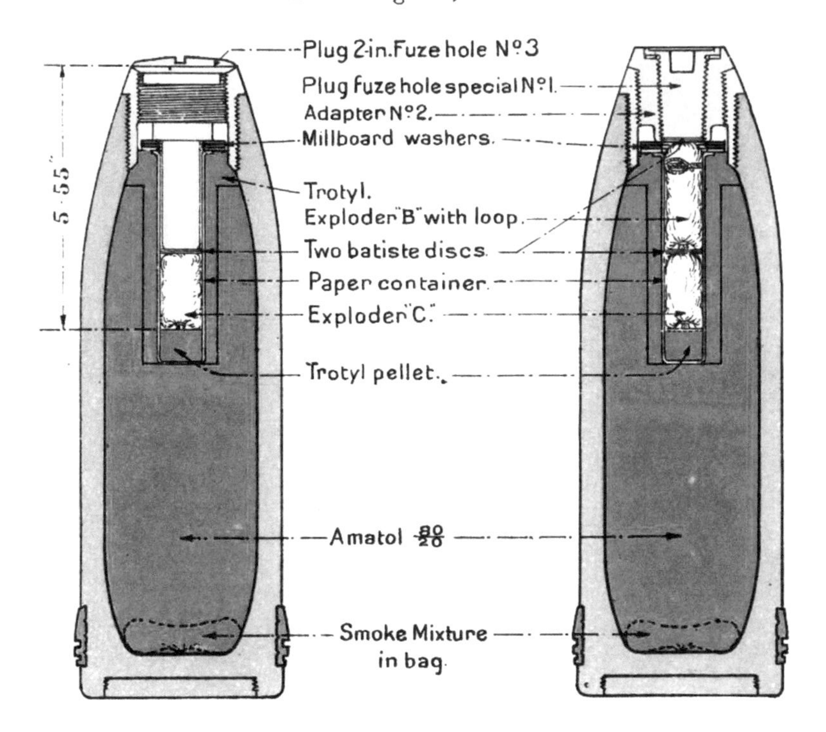

The filling shewn above for amatol cold pressed or hot mixed is typical of the later methods of shell filling. The explosive in the form of a powder is pressed into the shell with suitable punches to the required density, or screw filled, a much larger cavity being left than in the earlier designs. Into this cavity two cylinders of trotyl are placed, or the cavity is filled by poured or pressed trotyl and in the centre a thick paper container is inserted, round the top of which, trotyl or other approved composition is poured to a specified level. This completely seals the explosive from the effects of damp.

For the purpose of locating bursts, smoke mixture either loose at the bottom of the cavity, or in a bag, is placed in shell to this design.

Method of Filling Shell, H.E., 4·5-in. and above.

R.L. Design 23,894 A–C.

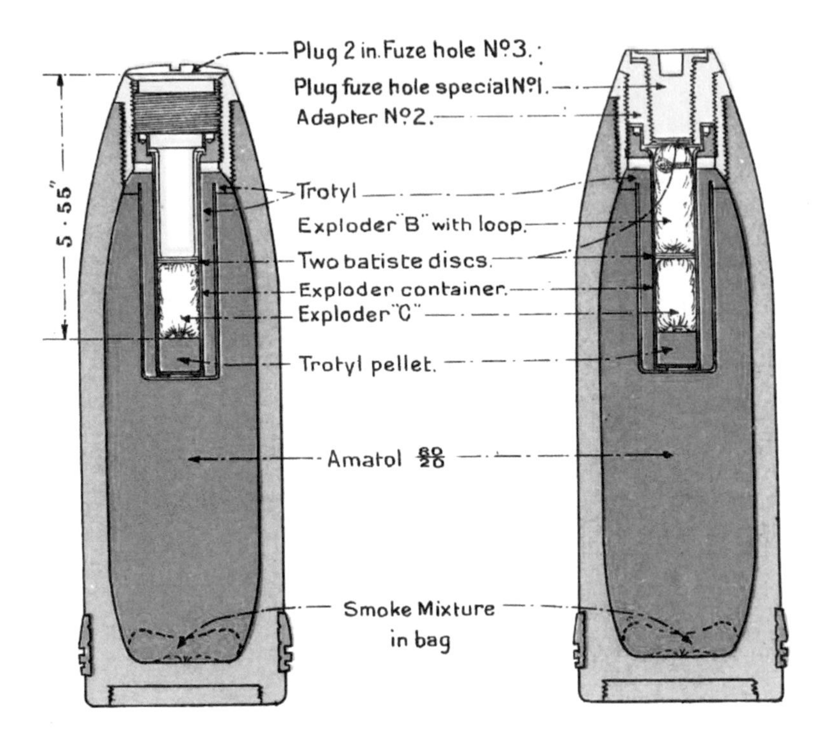

This filling for amatol cold pressed or hot mixed only differs from that described on the previous page by the substitution of a steel exploder container for one of paper. This has been introduced with the object of sealing the charge and preventing exudation.

For the purpose of locating bursts, smoke mixture, either loose at the bottom of the cavity or in a bag, is placed in shell to this design.

Method of Filling & Fuzing Shell, H.E.

R.L. Design 23,894.A

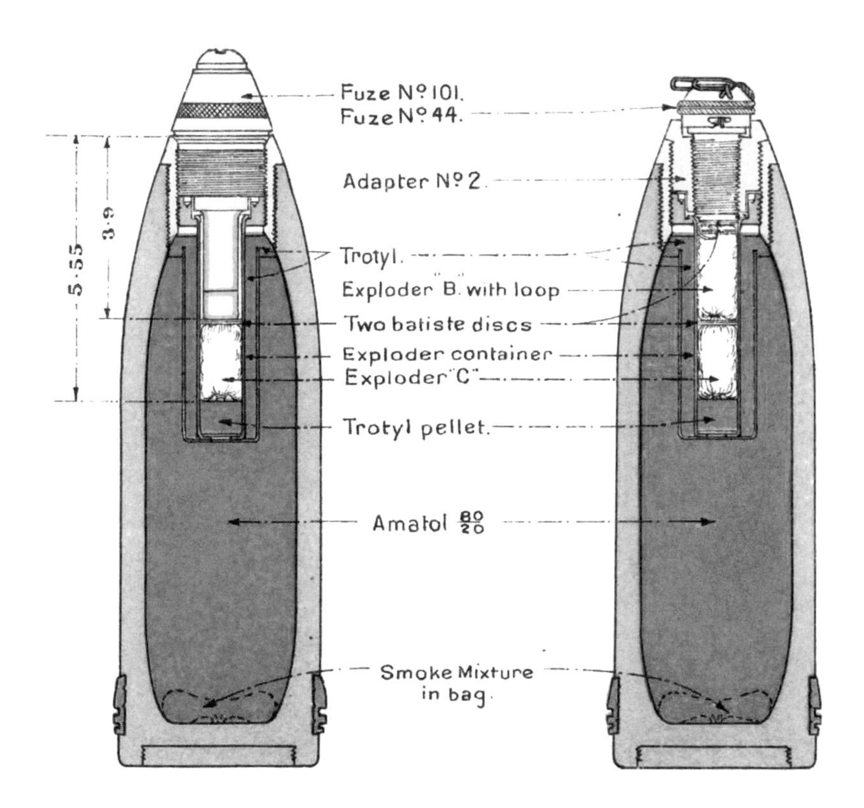

This is the same filling as shewn on page 3 but with the shell fuzed, in one case with Fuze No. 101 and Gaine No, 2, and in the other with Fuze No. 44, with which an additional exploder is needed. Fuze No. 101 is locked in the shell and prevented from working loose by "setting down" a portion of the thin lip on the body of the fuze into a nick in the mouth of the shell. Fuze No. 44 is self-locking owing to the taper of the fuze hole. No. 106 fuze requires exploders similar to No. 44 fuze, but does not require the adapter.

Instructions for Fuzing H.E. Shell, 4·5-in. How. & above

A. Shells with G.S. Fuze Holes.
Remove the plug and insert the fuze.

B. Shells with 2-inch Fuze Holes.

1. If issued plugged with a 2-inch plug.
   (a) If to be fuzed with a No. 100, 101, or 102 fuze, remove the plug and screw in the fuze with gaine.

IMPORTANT—READ CAREFULLY.

Special Instructions for Fuzing No. 100.

1. See that the plug immediately below the red mark is well home

and not likely to foul the threads of the shell when the fuze is being screwed home. If the plug is not home, the fuze should be returned to store. The plug should not on any account be touched.

2. When the fuze has been inserted in the shell, care should be taken to ensure that the red mark on the fuze is not above the set screw in the shell. If the red mark is in this position the fuze should be exchanged, as tightening up the set screw might explode the shell.

3. If the fuzed shell is not required to be travelled, there is no need to insert the set screw, but care must be taken to see that the red mark on the fuze is not opposite the set screw hole in the shell and that the fuze is screwed home in the shell before firing.

(*b*) If to be fuzed with a No. 106 fuze, remove the plug and insert, choke downwards, the "B" exploder (16 drams nominal) which is supplied with the fuze, pressing it gently into place in the shell cavity with the thumb. Insert the fuze and screw it home.

(*c*) If to be fuzed with a G.S. fuze, remove the plug, screw in the adapter, and insert an exploder, choke downwards. The exploder to be "B" (16 drams nominal) in the case of No. 44 fuze, and "D" (10 drams nominal) in the case of No. 18 or 45 fuzes. Screw in the fuze.

2. If issued with an adapter and plugged with a G.S. plug.

(*a*) If to be fuzed with a 2-inch gauge fuze, remove the plug and adapter, remove the upper exploder by means of its loop and proceed as in 1 (*a*) or (*b*).

(*b*) If to be fuzed with a G.S. fuze, remove the plug and insert the fuze, noting by reference to the shell marking that the exploders under the fuze are as specified in 1 (*c*) above.

NOTE :—Where shell are fitted with fixing screws, the latter must be screwed back before the plug or adapter can be removed, and should be screwed on to fuze or adapter after fuzing. Future supplies of shell will not have set screws, the insertion of such screws being unnecessary in the case of shell fuzed just before firing (in the case of shell issued fuzed special provision is made for securing the fuze or adapter to withstand transit).

The insertion of fuzes and adapters may be facilitated by coating the threads of the fuze or adapter with a little No. 3 luting, thinned down with a little mineral jelly.

If the shell is likely to be stored sometime before firing, it is advisable to smear the under side of the lip, just above the screw thread on the fuze or adapter, with a small fillet of unthinned No. 3 luting, before inserting the fuze or adapter into the shell, excess of luting being wiped off after the fuze or adapter is home.

Method of Filling Shell, H.E., 18-pr. and below.

R.L. Designs various.

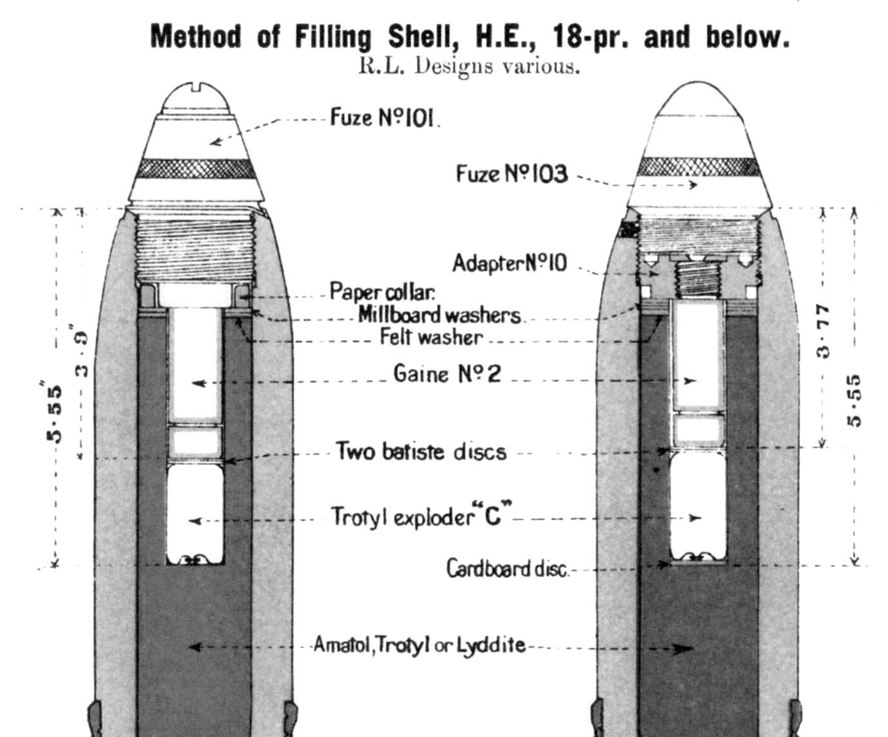

The illustrations above shew typical methods of filling and fuzing shell 18-pr. and below. The explosive charge may be inserted in the form of a block or blocks, or as a poured filling, or a pressed filling. In each case, a cavity is left to take the gaine and exploder. The exploder is then inserted, compressed to a specified length, and two batiste discs are placed on the top of it. After putting a felt washer on the surface of the filling, millboard washers are inserted to within a fixed distance from the mouth of the shell. When fuzing with No. 101 or 102 Fuze a paper collar is used to fill up the space round the adapter, and after screwing the fuze and gaine home into the shell a thin lip on the body of the fuze (if thus provided) is set down into one of the three nicks provided for the purpose, thus locking the fuze and preventing it from working loose. Fuzes not provided with a lip are secured by stabbing the fuze into the nicks in the shell or by means of a tinned plate washer locked into fuze and stabbed down into the shell. When shell are fuzed with No. 106 Fuze, two exploders are used. With No. 103 Fuze a separate adapter is used to carry the gaine and the slight difference in overall length as compared with that of No. 101 Fuze and gaine is made up by inserting a cardboard disc under the exploder.

Method of Filling Shell, H.E. 4-inch and below.

Anti-Aircraft.

R.L. Design 25529 A.

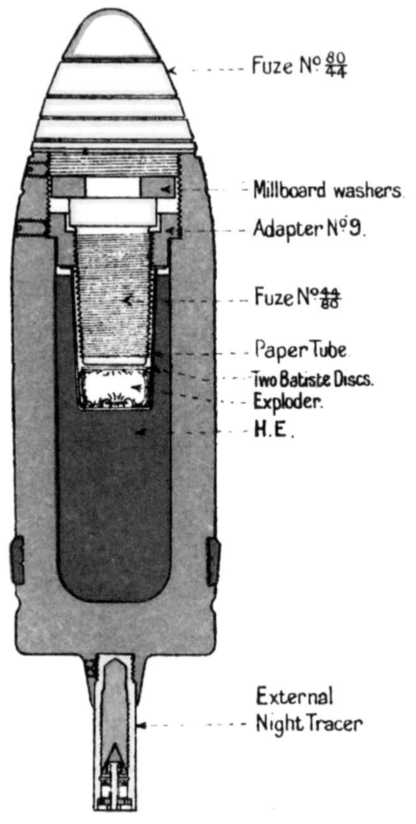

The above is a high explosive shell fitted with a night tracer for anti-aircraft work. A cavity is left in the filling to take the 44/80 D.A. fuze, which is carried in an adapter and above this is an 80/40 or other time fuze, *i.e.*, an 80 or other T. & P. fuze, which has had the percussion mechanism removed or rendered inoperative. When the time fuze functions, the flash from its magazine drives in the needle disc, firing the detonator and detonating the C.E. in the fuze and the bursting charge of the shell. Nos. 7 and 8 gaines are now coming into use in place of No. 44/80 fuzes, from which they differ by having the screw thread below the adapter replaced by a parallel plain portion. A.A. high explosive shell are also issued with No. 11 adapter (with shutter) and No. 2 gaine, in place of No. 9 adapter and No. 44/80 fuze.

For some time to come, A.A. shell will be issued without night tracers.

CHEMICAL SHELL.

Instructions regarding the use of Chemical Shell.

(Confidential).

These shells contain in the head an explosive charge only sufficient to open the shell effectively.

In woods, buildings or covered emplacements, the effect might be felt for a long time.

The radius of action of this type of shell depends almost entirely on atmospheric conditions, especially wind. The most favourable circumstances for use are when there is a total absence of wind, or a light breeze preferably blowing towards the enemy. Heavy rain, a strong wind or a temperature near freezing point minimize the effect.

Gas shells in store and during transport must be kept apart from other shells (separate trucks, cases, and so forth.) In the case of leakage from any shell, such a shell must be buried in the ground at a depth of not less than 3½ feet. It must not be thrown into water on account of danger of contaminating the latter.

The men in local or artillery stores, where the gas shells are kept, or men transporting such shells, and batteries who have to fire the gas shells, must be provided with anti-gas helmets of the "large box-respirator" type, which must be used only in cases of emergency as, for example, in the case of leakage from any shells.

For details of marking chemical shell see page Miscellaneous, 6.

Distinguishing colour bands round body of Chemical Shell :—

P.S.—1 white band.

C.B.R.—1 red band.

V.N.—1 white and 1 red band.

P.G.—2 white bands.

N.C.—1 white, 1 red, and 1 white band.

C.G.—1 red, 1 white, and 1 red band.

S.K.—No bands.

K.S.K.—No bands, but letters "H V Y" stencilled on body.

Shell, S.K., 4·5-in. Howitzer.

R.L. Design 23,316.

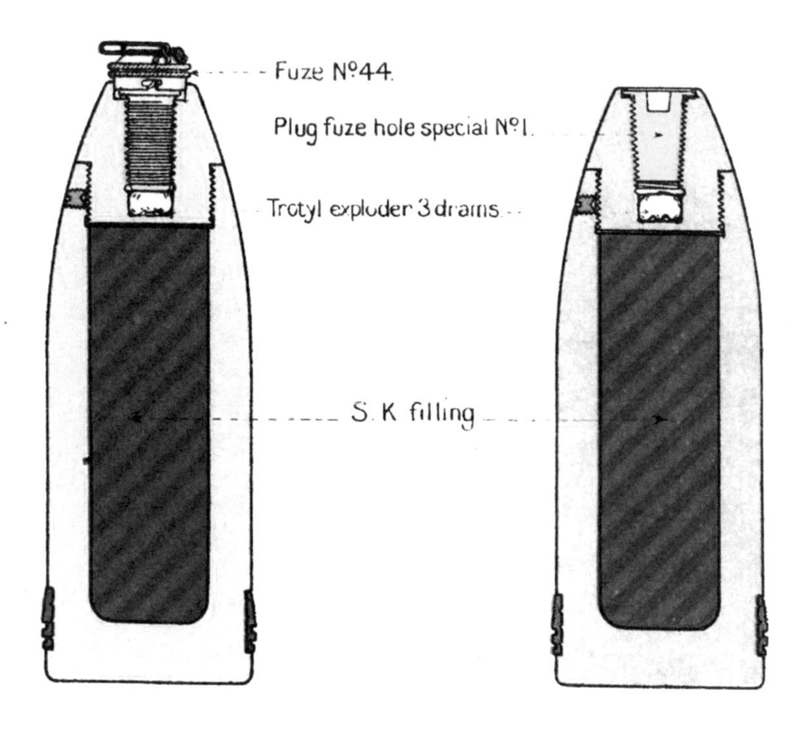

SHELL FUZED. SHELL PLUGGED

The above diagrams show an early type of chemical shell made of cast iron. The body of the shell contains the S.K. liquid, and the No. 44 Fuze and 3-dr. exploder carried in the head are sufficient to open the shell and scatter its contents.

Method of Filling Shell, Chemical, 60-pr.

R.L. Design 26,449

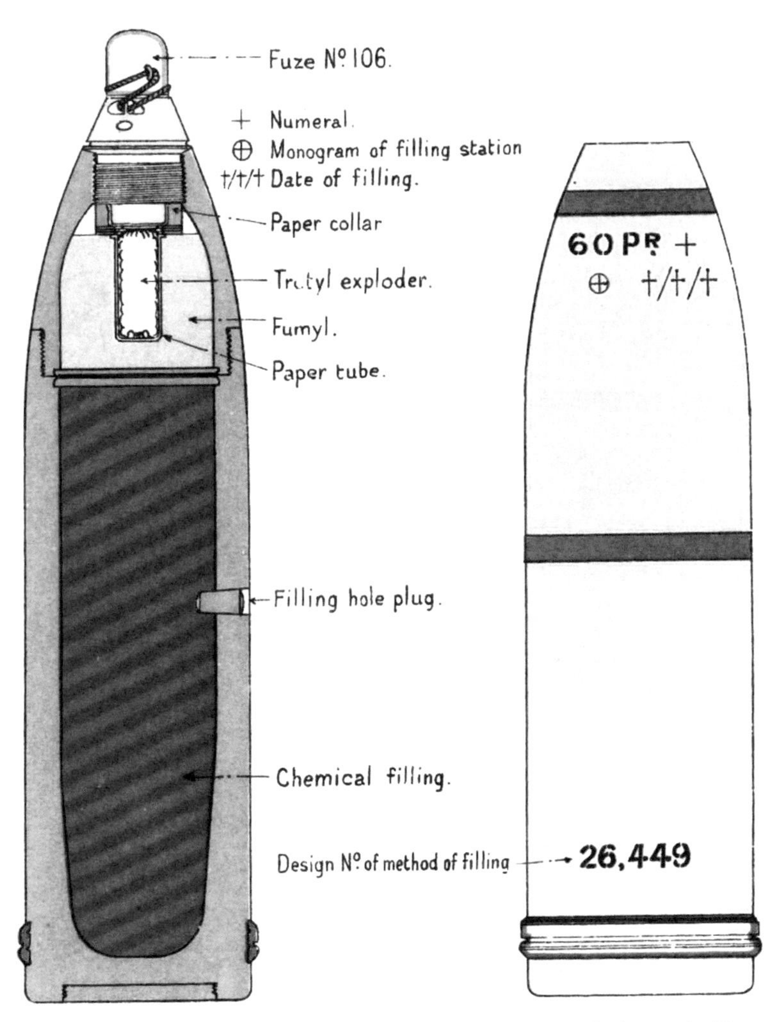

The above diagrams shew a chemical shell of the "double diaphragm" type. With these shell the explosive filling and the chemical filling can be carried out quite separately, the heads and bodies being assembled after they have been filled. The filling shewn in the head above, consists of an exploder compressed under the fuze and surrounded by a mixture of high explosive and smoke producing material (fumyl). A felt washer is placed on top of the filling, followed by millboard washers and a paper collar.

The diaphragms are rivetted in and the screw threads coated with cement to minimise the possibility of leakage. The filling hole and plug are slightly tapered to ensure a perfectly tight fit when the plug is driven in.

Method of Filling Shell, Chemical, 4·5-in. Howitzer,

R.L. Design 26,583.

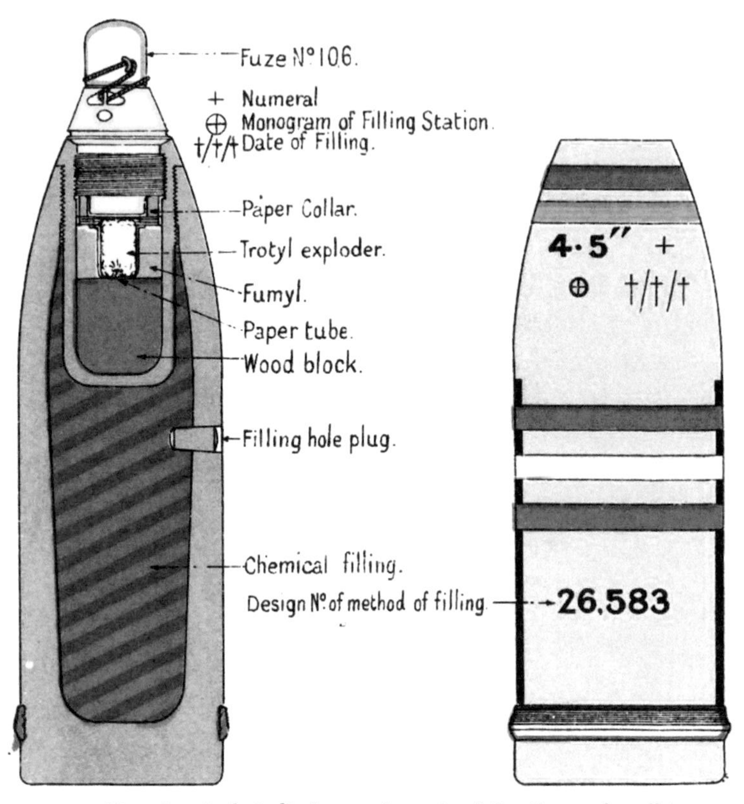

The chemical shell shewn above is of the "container" type and consists of a service H.E. shell or cast iron or semi-steel shell fitted with a steel container to carry the explosive and smoke producing mixture. A filling hole for the chemical is also provided. The container filling consists of a stemmed-in mixture of fumyl, a cavity being formed to take the exploder underneath a No. 44 or 106 fuze. Millboard washers and a paper collar are used to ensure a tight packing between the container filling and the adapter, and the joint is sealed with composition beeswax.

The threads of the container are coated with cement and the joint between container and shell caulked to minimise the possibility of leakage. The filling hole and plug are slightly taper to ensure a perfectly tight fit when the plug is driven in.

To adjust these shell to weight, blocks of cast iron or wood are used at the bottom of the container to ccunter-balance the variations in densities of the chemicals used. Lead shot is also used in small quantities in the chemical filled cavity with the same object.

Shell, B.L., Star, 6-inch Howitzer.

R.L. Design 10,359 K.

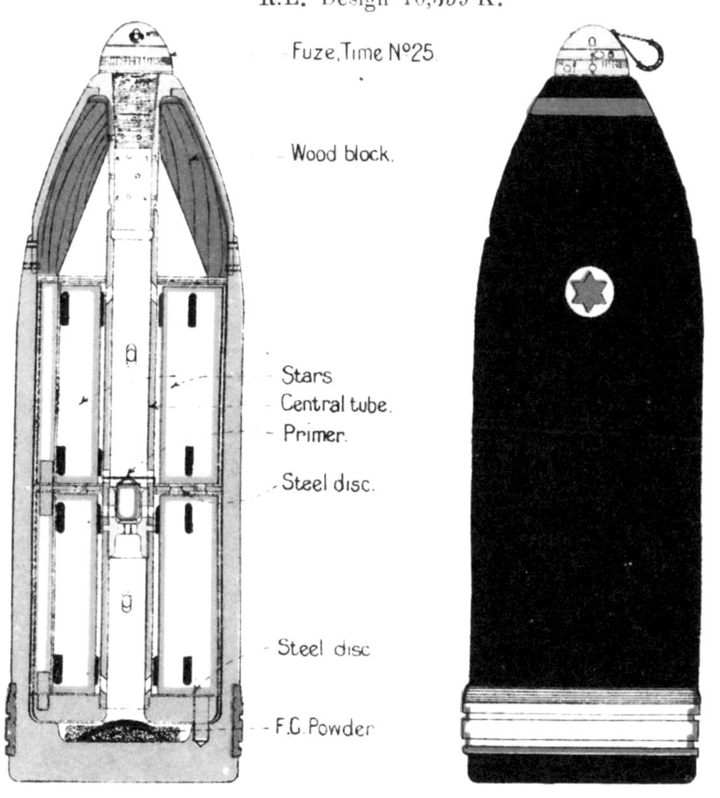

The star shell in the illustration is similar in many respects to a Shrapnel shell. As in the case of the latter, it carries a bursting charge in a recess in the base, a steel disc, a central tube, and has a removable head which is lightly secured to the body by steel screws and is fitted with twisting pins to enable it to take up the rotation of the body in flight. The shell contains twelve stars in two tiers of six, and these consist of paper cylinders into which is pressed star composition with a priming of mealed powder at each end and overhanging strands of quickmatch. The stars are supported on steel discs separated by corrugated steel distance pieces, and pins are provided which prevent rotation of disc and stars relative to the shell body. When the time fuze functions the flash ignites a primer, supported half way down the tube, which in its turn ignites the strands of quickmatch on the stars through holes in the central tube, and the bursting charge in the base. The latter is just sufficient to force off the head and release the burning stars from the body.

The above type of shell, which was used for various natures up to 6-inch, is now being superseded by star shell of the single star and parachute type, described and illustrated on page "Star Shell, 2."

Shell, B.L., Star, 6-inch Howitzer.

R.L. Design 26,057.

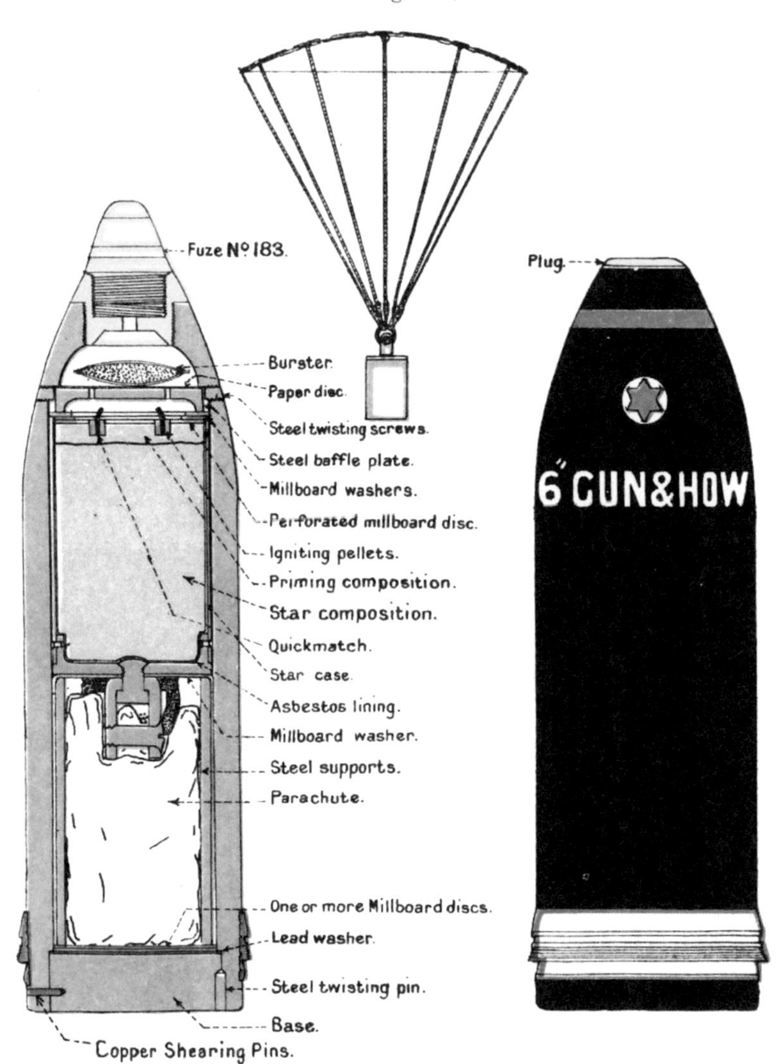

The star shell illustrated above is typical of the new type of parachute star shell now in use for guns and howitzers, 6-inch and below. The shell is fitted with a burster in the head, supported on a baffle plate which is made to rotate with the shell by means of twisting screws. Below the baffle plate is the star, consisting of a steel case filled with star composition with priming composition at the top, into which are set igniting pellets containing strands of quickmatch. To the bottom of the star case is fitted a swivel which forms the means of attachment for the parachute below. The latter is made of fabric strengthened by means of wire rope, and a series of wires are connected to a grummet which is attached to the star case swivel. The parachute is folded up and pressed into the shell, the base of which is closed by means of a steel base, fixed with copper shearing pins and prevented from rotating by means of a twisting pin. A lead washer makes the joint between the base and the shell. The set back of the star is taken on the base by means of a steel support in halves. The shell is fitted with a time or time and percussion fuze of the No. 80, 82, 83, or 85 type, which is set to give the required range.

Action.—On the fuze functioning at the set time, the magazine of the fuze ignites the powder burster below, which sets up sufficient pressure to shear the copper shearing pins and at the same time ignite the igniting pellets and priming composition of the star. The star and parachute are ejected from the base of the shell, and the parachute opens out, rights itself, and allows the flaring star to fall gradually to ground, open end downwards, as shewn in the inset view.

Shell, Q.F., Incendiary 4.5-inch Howitzer

R.L. Design 25,186.

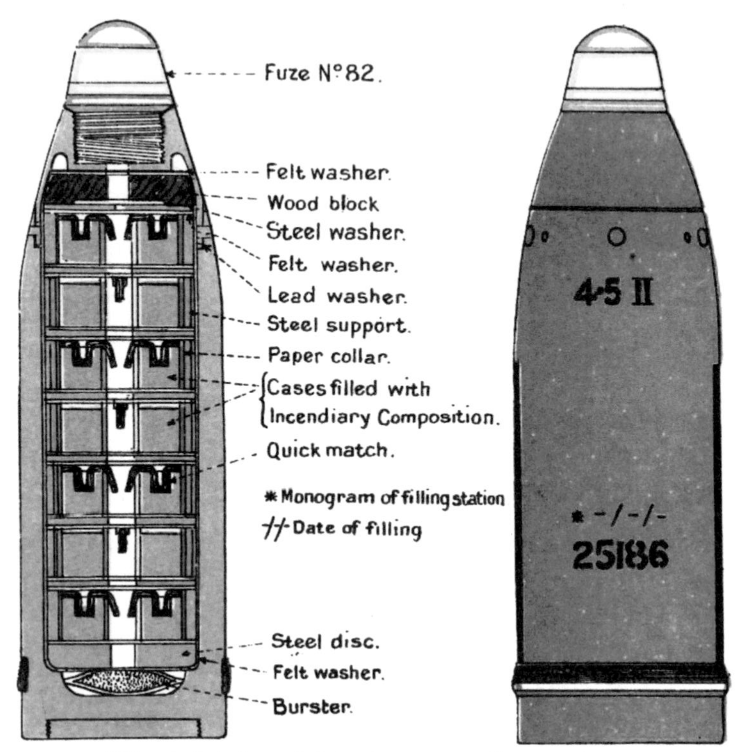

This shell is intended for incendiary effect against crops, undergrowth, houses, and inflammable material generally.

A bursting charge is placed in the bottom of the shell cavity, and on the ledge above is seated a steel disc bedded on a felt washer.

Seven incendiary cases are then assembled in the cavity, their weight being taken by steel supports ; paper collars are fitted to make a secure packing.

The head is then assembled (the joint being made with Pettman cement and a lead washer) and secured by screws and twisting pins.

Action.—The flash from the fuze passes through the hole in the wood block and steel washer, to the burster, and in doing so flashes down the central tubes of the incendiary cases into which project strands of quickmatch connected to the priming composition in the cases. The incendiary cases are thus ignited before the powder charge blows them out of the nose of the shell.

The incendiary cases are erratic in flight and the angle of opening gives a wide area of possible incendiary effect.

The setting of the fuze should be the same as for shrapnel, but not too long, as a low burst may cause the discs to be put out before they are well alight.

Description of and Instructions for the use of Q.F., Incendiary, A.Z. (Anti-Zeppelin) Shell.

(Filled D.W. Composition.)

This type of Incendiary A.Z. Shell has the base bored through and recessed to take a loose steel plug held in position by three copper shearing pins and a steel twisting pin. Into the bottom of the fuze hole is screwed a steel adapter, carrying a central tube.

Filling.—A millboard washer is placed on the underside of the adapter and the shell is filled from the base with a felt washer, followed by D.W. composition, finished off with a layer of powder priming and six holes formed, as shown, and filled with mealed powder. Two millboard washers (one inside the other) are then placed on the priming, the annulus between them being filled with slow rocket composition. A perforated steel support covered with a washer of primed shalloon is then inserted, and takes its seating on the end of the central tube. A millboard washer is placed next to the steel support and the base inserted and secured by means of the copper shearing pins and steel twisting pin, the joint being made by a lead washer above the flange on the base.

Action.—The flash from the fuze is transmitted through the central tube and ignites the small quantity of composition between the millboard washers. This fires the priming and the incendiary composition in the body. The base is blown out with the result that a flame is emitted through the base of the shell. This flame lasts for about 15 seconds and gives tracer effect.

The shell can be identified as follows :—

(1). The shell is painted **Red.** "**A.Z.**" and design number of filling are stencilled on the body.

(2). Package **Red** with letters "**A.Z.**" after nomenclature of shell.

The fuze to be used is **No. 180 or 185 with the percussion arrangement removed,** so as to prevent ignition or explosion on impact with the ground if the time portion of the fuze fails. The space between the bottom of fuze and steel adapter is to be filled with millboard washers. The setting of the time fuze should be four seconds shorter than the correct setting for time shrapnel.

N.B.—In view of this difference in the setting of the incendiary shell fuze it will be necessary for incendiary shell to be stored in the Ready Racks apportioned to fuze settings four seconds longer than the setting of the incendiary shell fuze, *i.e*, "Ready Racks apportioned to Shrapnel or H.E., set for 14, should contain Incendiary shell with fuzes set at 10."

It is essential that this ammunition be stored and transported separate from other ammunition. It is classed under **Group IV. Division I,** and will be issued **fuzed.**

For illustration of Q.F. Incendiary Shell see next page.

Shell, Q.F., Incendiary, A.Z., 75 m/m Gun. (for British Service).

R.L. Design 26,688 A.

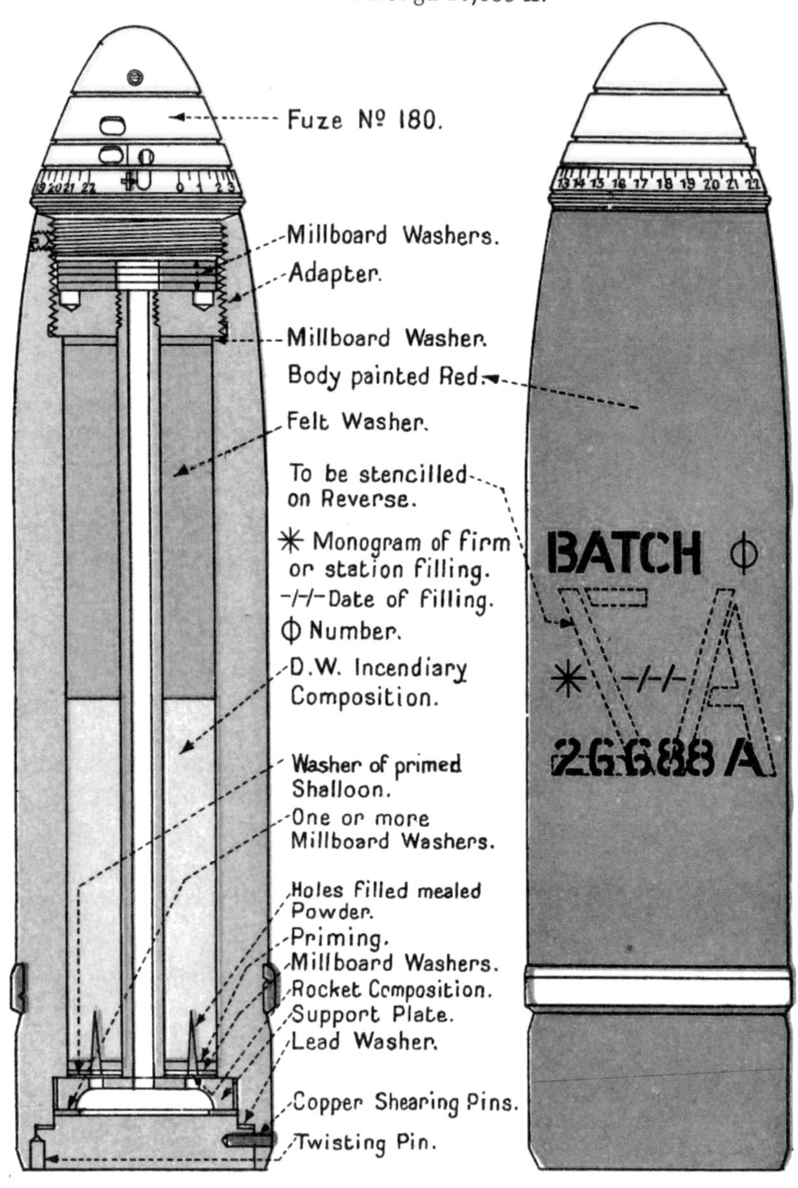

Method of Filling Shell, Smoke, 4·5-Inch Howitzer.

R.L. Design 27,268.

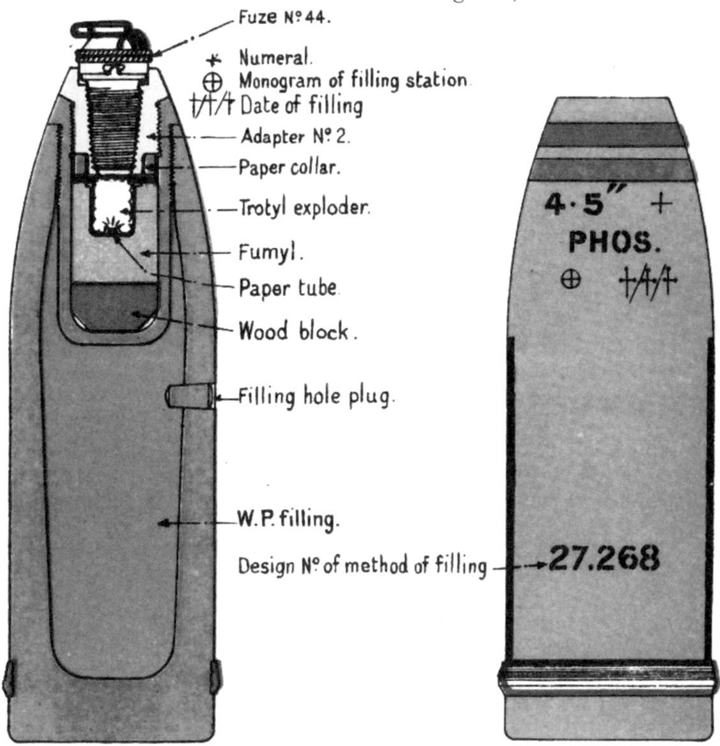

The smoke shell above consists of an H.E. type of shell fitted with a container to carry the bursting charge and having the body filled with white phosphorus. The phosphorus is filled in through the filling hole, which is afterwards closed by means of a tapered plug. The container filling consists of an exploder compressed below a No. 44 or 106 Fuze and surrounded by fumyl, *i.e.* similar to chemical shell.

Method of Filling Shell, 18-Pr. Smoke.

R.L. Design 25,018 A.

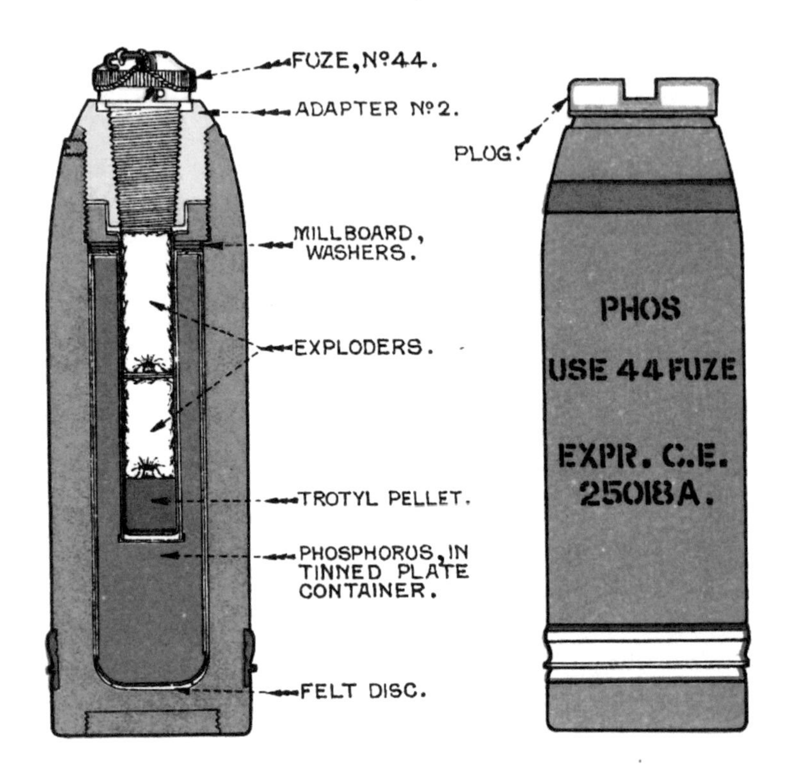

The above diagram shows an 18-pr. Smoke Shell. It consists of a modified H.E. shell body fitted with a container filled with white phosphorus and sealed up. The phosphorus container has a cavity in its upper end to accommodate an exploder container in which is the explosive charge. The fuze hole of the shell is fitted with an adapter which carries No. 44 fuze. No. 106 fuze has now been allocated to these shell, and will replace No. 44 fuze and adapter No. 2.

Method of Filling Shell, Shrapnel.

R.L. Design 21,747.

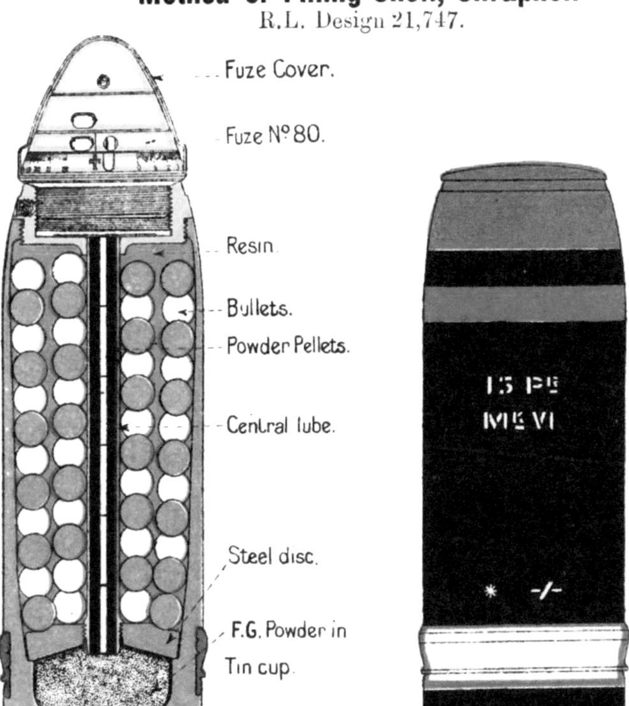

The above is a typical design of the smaller natures of Shrapnel shell. The steel body, which is made as light and thin as possible consistent with its ability to withstand shock of discharge from the gun, has a recess in the base which takes the tin cup containing the bursting charge, and above this a steel disc, resting on a ledge, of sufficient strength to support the bullets on "set back." A central tube screws into this disc and the annular space around it is filled with bullets embedded in resin. A metal socket, screwed to take the fuze, closes the mouth of the shell, the upper end of the central tube terminating in the base of this socket. The fuze is shewn fitted with a metal cover which can be stripped off to allow the setting of the fuze. The action of the shell is as follows :—

The time rings burn round according to the "setting" of the fuze and ignite the powder in the magazine, the flash from the latter passing down the central tube and igniting the bursting charge, which acting on the steel disc, drives the bullets, socket (or head) and fuze out of the shell. The bullets are scattered in the form of a cone. Larger natures of Shrapnel shell are fitted with separate heads, the connection between head and body only being sufficiently strong to keep the shell intact during transit and until the fuze functions. Smaller natures of Shrapnel shell have usually had powder pellets in the tube as shewn for increasing the angle of dispersion of bullets. These are now being omitted.

ND - #0450 - 270225 - C56 - 220/145/5 - PB - 9781908487599 - Matt Lamination